Chesapeake Bay

A PICTORIAL MARITIME HISTORY

A Virginia Pilot-Boat Getting Underway. Colored lithograph by J. Rogers, 1825, owned by The National Maritime Museum.

Chesapeake Bay

A PICTORIAL MARITIME HISTORY

By M. V. BREWINGTON

BONANZA BOOKS · NEW YORK

0-517-094371

COPYRIGHT MCMLIII, © MCMLVI

CORNELL MARITIME PRESS

Library of Congress Catalog Card Number: 53-9689

Printed in the United States of America

This edition published by Bonanza Books,
a division of Crown Publishers, Inc.,
by arrangement with Tidewater Publishers
A B C D E F G H

Table of Contents

" . . . the history and customs of such a people, preserved . . . by illustrations, are themes worthy of the lifetime of one man . . ."
George Catlin, 1840.

Preface

THIS is an attempt to assemble a portion of the wealth of pictures of events, objects, and vessels on and around Chesapeake Bay, and with a minimum of text let them tell the Bay's maritime story from its first settlement down to the present.

In pictorial records few areas of the United States have been so fortunate and no area holds more of maritime interest. Here the first permanent English settlement was made; here shipbuilding as a profession had its American beginnings; here the first of our purely local watercraft was developed. For a century and a half the Chesapeake's waters carried cargoes of greater value and bulk than all the rest of America combined. These waters saw the first naval engagement, the first amphibious expedition, and the action which altered the whole course of naval warfare. The list of firsts might be expanded indefinitely if space were available. Suffice to say the Bay had a major part in our national as well as local history and entered more or less directly into every phase of every life lived along its shores and well into the hinterlands of not only Virginia and Maryland but also New York, Pennsylvania, West Virginia, and North Carolina.

The pictures published here are by no means fortuitous finds; they have been sought for with some little background of what is needed to illustrate the maritime history of the Chesapeake. They represent far less than half of those available. In making the selection for publication a factual, realistic standard rather than an artistic one has ruled with a contemporaneous work given first choice when more than one picture of the same subject is to be had. Only one modern picture of an ancient event, the arrival of the Virginia colonists, has been included. No artist seems to have been present in 1607 and unlike so many of our historical paintings Commander Coale's research has been proved not disproved by subsequent discoveries. There are a number of gaps in the pictorial record, particularly in the events of the Seventeenth Century which it is hoped new finds and identifications will fill. Because the conduct of trade in Canton, Callao, or London was the same with either a New York, Boston, or Bay owned vessel, no attempt has been made to include pictures of foreign ports even if Bay traders dominated the scene as they did in some African and South American ports.

The task involved in printing a book of this nature is certainly not a simple one. I have handed the printer copies of oil paintings, watercolors, engravings, lithographs, daguerreotypes, and photographs dating from 1585 to 1953. To give some semblance of unity to such a heterogeneous group doubtless has tried all the technical skills of the engraver and pressman and given the master printer more than his share of headaches. To them my thanks.

M. V. BREWINGTON.

Dorothy's Discovery,
Cambridge, Maryland
May 1953.

Acknowledgements

THE SOURCE from which each picture is derived is given with the reproduction. But the mere name of a person or an institution cannot fully acknowledge my debt for the troubles taken in my behalf. More fully I wish to express my appreciation for pictures and special information to:

R. C. Anderson

George Barrie, Jr.

John Branford

Alexander C. Brown

Robert H. Burgess

Charles H. P. Copeland

Clinton De Witt

Ernest S. Dodge

John G. Earle

Louis Feuchter

James W. Foster

Richard Goldsborough

W. Avery Hall

Frederick F. Hill

H. Robbins Hollyday

W. H. Hunter

C. Lowndes Johnson

John L. Lochhead

Captain Otis Lloyd

Frank A. Moorshead

Cdr. W. E. May, R.N.

H. Osborne Michael

A. Pierce Middleton

Harry Shaw Newman

G. H. Pouder

Morris Radoff

William T. Radcliffe

M. S. Robinson

E. J. Rousuck

Henry Rusk

Fred Shelley

B. Frank Sherman

R. A. Skelton

Harold Sniffen

Raymond Spears

W. C. Steuart

Edward Stewart

Colton Storm

Frank A. Taylor

H. Graham Wood

Frank A. Moorshead, Jr.

List of Illustrations

I.

The Explorers and Settlers

IN 1585 a band of Englishmen under Sir Ralph Lane started on foot from Sir Walter Raleigh's colony at Roanoke in search of a great inland sea the Indians had described. Their thoughts were of a North West Passage to the Indies. After many days in the wilderness they reached the banks of what may have been the Elizabeth River or perhaps Lynnhaven Bay where they found an Indian tribe named the *Chesepiuc*. Although Lane may not have seen the Bay proper, when his explorations were mapped, he gave the name of the Indian tribe to the great Bay—*Chesapeake,* meaning some say, "Mother of Waters," while others translate it "Country on a great water." When Wright and Molyneaux drew their famous world map, the first on Mercator's projection, they copied the name and thereafter it has remained.

Even if Lane had reached the Bay, he would not have been the first white man to do so. As early as 1573 the Spaniards had actually prepared sailing directions for entering the Capes, calling the Bay *Baia de Santa Maria,* and a settlement was made somewhere on the banks of the James River. It was short lived and not until 1607 did a colony find permanent root. This was the Virginia Company's Jamestown.

Almost at once the colonists began to explore the nearby lands and streams. Captain John Smith, one of its leaders, made a "discovery" of the waters which extended over the horizon to the northward of James River. For sixty days he and a few companions sailed and rowed an open boat landing and searching the back country in hopes of finding precious metals or the North West Passage. As they progressed they named the rivers, islands, and other topographic features for the settlers or the Indian tribes they met, and when the party returned to Jamestown, Smith drew a map of the region. It was published in England in 1612 and although Smith missed seeing several of the most important rivers flowing into the

Bay, for nearly a century his Map served as the basis for many of the charts drawn for the navigation of the Chesapeake.

By the time Lord Baltimore's colonists arrived in 1634 fur traders from Virginia had become thoroughly acquainted with all the Bay's waters and had even opened trading posts, one on Kent Island and another on Palmer's Island in the Susquehanna River mouth. Had these traders measured accurately they would have found 4612 miles of tidal shore line and 48 principal rivers. "Into these Rivers run an abundance of great creeks or short Rivers [102 of them] navigable for Sloops, Shallops, Long-Boats, Flats, Canoes and Periaguas" wrote Hugh Jones in 1724. Continuing he said, "These Creeks are supplied with Tides (which indeed does not rise so high as in Europe, so prevents their making good Docks) and also with fresh-water runs replenished with Branches issueing from the Springs and soaking through the Swamps; so that no country is better watered for the conveniency of which most Houses are built near some Landing-Place; so that any Thing may be delivered to a Gentleman there from London, Bristol & C with less trouble and Cost, than to one living five miles in the Country in England."

While two centuries were to pass before the Bay was completely and accurately charted, the exploratory period might be said to have passed by the time the Maryland settlement was established at St. Mary's City.

DIRECTIONS
FOR
Virginia and Mary-Land.

SUCH as are bound for *Virginia* or *Mary-Land*, shall find many times on that Coast of *America* various Winds and Weather, and Streams, and Currents also, therefore the more Care, and not trust with too much Confidence to Dead Reckoning.

For by Experience hath been found sometimes in 24 hours, such Currents, as have carried them either to the Northward or Southward, contrary to their Reckoning, beyond Credit.

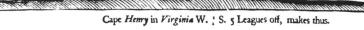

Cape *Henry* in *Virginia* W. ¦ S. 5 Leagues off, makes thus.

The first printed English sailing directions for the Chesapeake from *The English Pilot*, London, 1689, in The British Museum.

The arrival of the colonists off Jamestown, 1607. Ship *Godspeed*, 40 tons, Captain Bartholomew Gosnold; ship *Susan Constant*, 100 tons, Captain Christopher Newport; pinnace *Discovery*, 20 tons, Captain John Ratcliffe. Study by Griffith Baily Coale, 1948, at The Mariners' Museum, for the mural in the Virginia State Capitol.

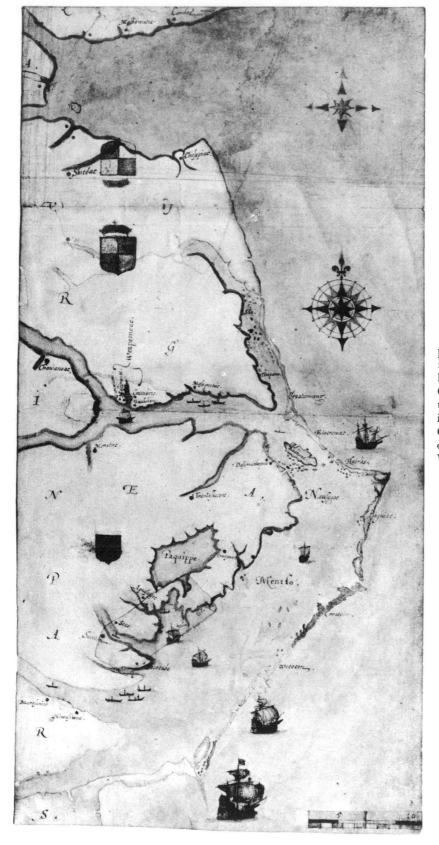

Sir Ralph Lane's exploration from Roanoke, 1585. The first known use of the name Chesapeake is given between the two streams indicated just inside Cape Henry. Water colored drawing by John White, ca. 1585, in The British Museum.

Map of Virginia by Captain John Smith. The earliest map of any accuracy covering the entire Chesapeake Bay Country. What is evidently the boat in which Smith explored the Bay is shown above Powel's [Poole's] Island. The first issue of the engraved map, Oxford, 1612, owned by The William L. Clements Library.

Captain John Smith, the first English explorer and cartographer of Chesapeake Bay. From the first issue of the engraved portrait owned by The William L. Clements Library.

The ship *Ark,* 300 tons, which brought over the Maryland colonists in 1634.

The pinnace *Dove,* 50 tons, consort of the *Ark.* These two reliefs in plaster, at Hook House, Wiltshire, England, the home of Lord Baltimore, are the only known contemporary representations of vessels which brought colonists to English North America. Photographs at The Maryland Historical Society.

An English manuscript chart of the American coast dated 1676 owned by
The National Maritime Museum.

II.

Shipbuilding

A S SOON as the first colonists reached Virginia they put
together a barge which had been brought out from England
in knockdown form. This was the first watercraft known to have
been built by Anglo-Saxons in the Bay Country. It should have been
followed by other small craft at least, for small craft were needed
and the colonists found ample materials close at hand: oak, pine,
and cedar, were plentiful and they soon learned that naval stores,
iron, and hemp for cordage could be produced. In fact all that was
necessary were experienced carpenters. These were sent out with
Sir Thomas Gates in 1610: 2 shipwrights, 20 shipcarpenters, 10
caulkers, 2 sparmakers, 4 smiths, and 2 ropemakers. They found 2
boats, 2 pinnaces, and 1 canoe and seemingly did little to add to the
number or even keep those in good condition for when Sir Samuel
Argoll arrived two years later he was forced to put his crew at work
making repairs in order to provide the colonists with some boats.
Then he built a "stout shallop," a "Frigot" and a "fishing Boate."
Again a band of carpenters, twenty-five this time, were sent out from
England under a master shipwright and again a beginning was made,
but most of the men died having been fed "corupte victualls" on
the way over. There were only forty boats in the whole colony in
1624, the largest a "barque" of forty tons.

Actually there was little need for the colonists to build or own
large vessels. Their chief product, tobacco, was in such demand
abroad that the English, and especially the Dutch merchants were
only too glad to send over vessels to take the tobacco to Europe,
trading their manufactured goods for it. One small group of colonists,
the Indian traders, did need craft of medium size since they made
extended trips up the Bay and its tributaries to their customers'
villages. They built their own vessels to a large degree. Captain
Henry ffleet, for instance, in 1632 built a shallop and a "Barque"
of 16 tons for his own use and Captain William Claiborne in 1634

had one William Paine running a shipyard on Kent Island turning out pinnaces and shallops for his trading activities. This was the first known yard in what became Maryland.

The construction of large vessels around the Bay had its real beginning in the last half of the Seventeenth Century following a series of great catastrophies in Europe and the Bay country which reduced the amount of world shipping to such a degree that few vessels came to the Bay for the tobacco crop. The shortage of bottoms plus a series of subsidy acts made ship owning profitable, particularly if home built. By 1697 a census of vessels built in Maryland since 1689 shows the industry on a firm foundation at last. While small craft still dominated in numbers, sea-going vessels as large as 450 tons were being built for English as well as local owners. There were listed 13 ships, 6 pinks, 12 brigantines, 66 sloops, 55 shallops, and 8 unspecified; 93 had been built on the Eastern Shore and 67 on the Western. In the Virginia report of that same year she owned 2 ships, 4 brigantines, and 9 sloops and had built 8 ships, 11 brigantines, and 15 sloops, with all the rigging, iron, sails, and even the carpenters coming out from England. The numbers of small craft are not given.

Notable by its absence from each census is the schooner. It appeared early in the next century and soon became the favorite for both Bay and Ocean uses. In the hands of the Bay builders it was developed into what eventually became known as the "Baltimore Clipper." Speed was its prime quality and every service which required that quickly adopted it; pilot-boats, slavers, privateers, dispatch-boats. At the same time burdensome vessels designed for carrying bulk cargoes, especially tobacco in its more or less standardized hogsheads, were being built in increasing numbers, many on speculation for sale in England after carrying over a cargo.

Until the use of metal for hulls became a major factor, shipbuilding continued to be a widespread industry with small yards near a good supply of timber turning out all classes of vessels by almost the same methods the first colonists had known. The production peak, exclusive of canal boats, came in the early 1830's when the Baltimore Clipper type of hull reached the height of its development, for example the ship *Ann McKim*, built at Baltimore in 1832 by Kennard and Williamson. An able marine reporter and critic who saw the *Ann McKim* at a Baltimore wharf in 1839 commented upon her beauty, her speed, and her lack of cargo capacity and contrasted her with a ". . . splendid new ship, recently launched, built on a somewhat new model under the direction of her owner, Captain Leslie, of this city. The vessel is called the *Scotia*, measuring 400 tons but capable of carrying 1200 at least. The character of Baltimore for building clippers has been celebrated in former days. Such vessels sacrifice burden to speed. The *Scotia* is the first vessel constructed on a new model combining the Baltimore and Boston systems, so as to unite burden and speed. It is calculated that the commercial interests of Baltimore have lost $5,000,000 during the last ten years, arising from the peculiar construction of their vessels. A complete revolution is begun. The *Scotia* is the first on the new plan . . . Ship building is carried on to a considerable extent here, and many merchants from the North have their vessels built here, principally from the superior cheapness of labor as compared with New York."

The great shipbuilding boom which followed the War of 1812 showed conclusively that America's supply of ship timber was far from inexhaustible. The Navy to insure a source had bought up the best stands of live oak, and timber buyers from the shipyards of New York and New England as well as Baltimore began to scour the Atlantic seaboard for compass timber for frames, stems, hooks, and knees. In the Bay country they found stands of white oak of the best quality. At first the shipbuilders sent down gangs of axe men equipped with rough moulds to which the timbers were hewed in the woods, then dragged by oxen to tidewater to be shipped in schooners to the builder's yard. In this way the frames of many of the famous New York Clippers of the 1850's came out of Maryland and Virginia woods. Soon the Bay's own lumbermen learned what was wanted and sent to the Down East yards rough sawn timbers which could be finished to shape on arrival. Even in the 1890's one Dorchester County timber dealer was furnishing complete frames to Baltimore shipbuilders. In addition to the oak, rafts of pine, yellow from the Maryland and Virginia rivers and white from up the Susquehanna, were poled down stream to local mills and even towed to Baltimore for planking, decks, and spars.

But the end of wooden ship construction had already been fore-shadowed. Almost a decade before the peak had been reached the first iron hull built in America, that of the steamboat *Codorus*, had been assembled and launched into one of the main tributaries of the Bay. When steam powered machinery for working wood and metals was introduced, capital greater than most of the Bayside yards could provide was necessary and soon shipbuilding became centered in a few large companies. Some of the minor yards, their output chiefly pleasure craft or making repairs to small commercial craft, have remained in business. On the Eastern Shore and in Virginia the watermen have always built the canoes, skiffs, and motor boats for their own use and perhaps a few for sale. That practise continues; most of their work, however, has lost all of its Bay character and only occasionally does one find a builder who is turning out the local types.

Facilities for ship repairs, particularly those requiring under-water work, were completely lacking until 1828 when a "screw dock" was built at Baltimore and in 1833 a stone dry dock was opened at the Gosport (Norfolk) Navy Yard. Prior to them a vessel needing bottom repairs had to be "hove down" in shallow water, a procedure which seldom failed to strain the hull to some degree. By the end of the Civil War several companies doing nothing except repair work were organized, a practise of specialization which grew as new construction became more and more centered in a few yards.

Once a Virginia or a Maryland built vessel was instantly recognized wherever she might be "by the cut of her jib." The local trade marks have disappeared, but the Chesapeake is still one of the greatest of American shipbuilding centers. Its three major yards are not only among the largest producers numerically; they have also turned out the longest and fastest ore carriers on the Great Lakes and many of the biggest seagoing cargo vessels and the fastest of all passenger liners.

The pinnace *Virginia* built 1607 from a plan of Fort St. George in the Archives at Simancas, Spain.

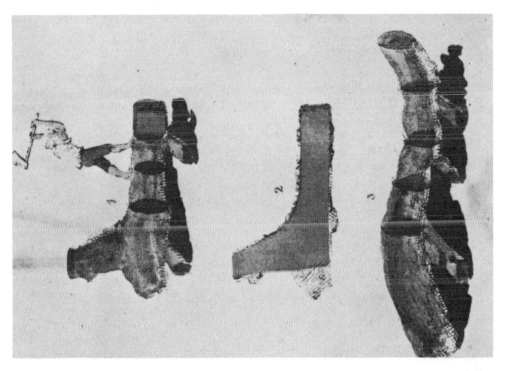

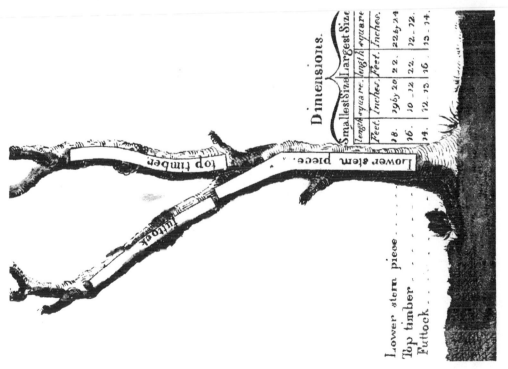

Dimensions.			
	Length square	Smallest Size	Largest Size
	Feet.	Inches.	Feet.	Inches.
Lower stern piece	18.	19 by 20	22.	22 by 24
Top timber	16.	10 _ 12	22.	22 _ 22.
Futlock	14.	12 _ 13	16.	13 _ 14.

Instructions on cutting ship timber. Lithograph by Henry Stone for Peter Gillet: *The Timber Merchants Guide*, Baltimore, 1823.

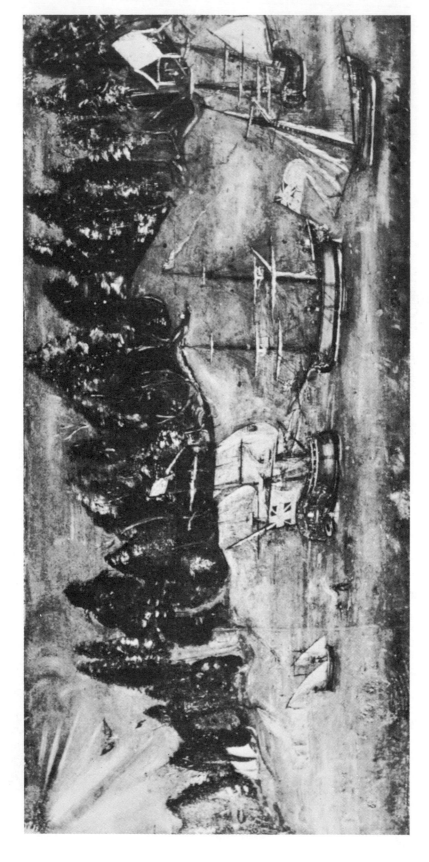

Spencer Hall Shipyard, Gray's Inn Creek, Kent County, Maryland, ca. 1760. The earliest known view of a Bay shipyard. In the background is the timber supply with lumbermen at work, the owner's home, a spar shed, and on the stocks two vessels under construction.

In the foreground almost every type of sea-going and Bay craft is depicted: a canoe, a large ship, the *Starling* (*Sterling?*), either a brig or a snow, a large sloop, two schooners, another small sloop, and several small boats. Oil painting on a wooden mantle panel owned by The Maryland Historical Society.

Fardy & Auld Shipyard, Baltimore, Maryland, ca. 1850. In many respects similar to the Spencer Hall yard in equipment, but the owner no longer lives in the yard and there is no local timber supply. Workmen are dragging timber ashore from a raft; others are hewing out shapes with broadaxe and adze; a pit-saw is in use getting out planks. Both new construction and repair work are underway. Oil painting attributed to W. Hare, owned by The Peale Museum.

The Chesapeake Marine Railway & Dry Dock Company, Baltimore, ca. 1868. A great change has taken place in two decades. Sawed pine lumber is coming in by canal boat, probably from the Pennsylvania forests and oak by timber cart. Steam power is available. A means for hauling vessels from the water is at hand. No new construction, only repair work, is shown. Lithograph owned by The Peale Museum.

Thomas Booz & Brother Shipyard, Baltimore, Maryland, ca. 1870. A yard specializing in new construction. Right, the brick building is the office, the frame building the saw shed with a mould loft above; center is the steam box for making plank pliable; in the background two unidentified vessels on the stocks. Photograph owned by The Peale Museum.

Newport News Shipbuilding and Dry Dock Company, Newport News, Virginia, 1906. Drydock number 2 with three, four, five, six, and seven masted schooners under repair. Photograph owned by The Mariner's Museum.

Bethlehem Steel Company, Sparrows Point Shipyard, Baltimore, Maryland, 1950. The largest integrated shipyard on the Bay, manufacturing its own steel, rolling plates, and building every type of vessel. Photograph from The Bethlehem Steel Company.

John Branford's shipyard, Fishing Island, Maryland, 1898. The skipjack *Annie Bennett* under construction. A small yard which built bugeyes, skipjacks, canoes, and crab skiffs, with all the work done by hand. Photograph owned by M. V. Brewington.

James T. Marsh's shipyard, Solomon's Island, Maryland, 1901. The bugeye *Nora Phillips* under construction and two bugeyes and a skipjack hauled out on the railways for repair. A small steam engine supplied power for the railways and the wood-working machinery. Photograph by George Barrie, Jr.

Thomas Kirby's shipyard, St. Michaels, Maryland, 1906. One of the larger Bay-side yards, founded 1868. It was equipped with steam power for tools, but the railway was operated by a horse treadmill. Photograph by Thomas Sewall.

Carl Smith's shipyard, Shad Point, Salisbury, Maryland, 1940. A small repair yard with all work done by hand, even the railway operated by man or horse power. Photograph by M. V. Brewington.

Otis Lloyd's shipyard, Salisbury, Maryland, 1906. In the foreground a tow-boat stern motor boat and in the background the round stern bugeye *Rebecca McLain* are under construction. Photograph by Raymond Spears.

His Majesty's frigate *Thetis* careened at Gosport, Virginia, shows the method of making underwater repairs before dry docks or railways existed on the Bay. Water color by Captain George Tobin, R.N., 1795, owned by The National Maritime Museum.

Backyard-built boats go to water by ox team.   Photograph by C. Lowndes Johnson.

Lumber raft on the way to Baltimore. Pencil drawing by J.H.B. Latrobe in F. Lucas, Jr.: *Progressive Drawing Book.*

A floating saw mill, ca. 1900, on Sassafras River, Maryland. Photograph by Thomas P. Hammer.

The Sheet Iron Steam Boat.
made by Davis. and Garchier,
the took it when it was dune
to the river Susquehanna,

The first iron hulled vessel built in the United States, the steamboat *Codorus*, 1825. Water color by Lewis Miller at The Historical Society of York County, Pennsylvania.

The steamship *United States*, built by Newport News Shipbuilding and Dry Dock Company, 1952. Photograph by William T. Radcliffe.

The Baltimore shipbuilder Joseph Despeaux (who died 1820) and his son John.
Oil painting owned by The Maryland Historical Society.

III.

Sailing Vessels

HAD Captain John Smith stepped aboard a ship in 1707 he would have found very little difference between her and the vessel on which he had come to Virginia a century before. The decks at the ends would not have been quite so high proportionately above water; she would have had more sail area; topgallants would be commonplace and perhaps royals might have been found on the fore and main masts and topgallants on the mizzen; she would have had a jib along with the square head-sails; and certainly she would have had more beam for the greater stowage of tobacco casks.

In the smaller craft more prominent changes would have occurred: to the single sail on each mast of the *Discovery* there would have been added topsails, topgallants, a lateen spanker and jibs. Sloops and ketches would be on the Bay and along the Coast. The old square-headed spritsail would have been forgotten. And within a few years (if not already there) the schooner would appear: a rig the like of which Captain John Smith had never seen, one dependent primarily not on square but on fore-and-aft sails. This was a far more efficient rig in working to windward and needed a smaller crew to handle it. Time showed it could be expanded from two to three to four and even more masts without loss of efficiency or economy. It would be the rig which would dominate the American inshore scene to the end of sail. Save on the schooner Smith would have been able to take command without difficulty.

But at about the same time the schooner appeared ship design in general threw off its lethargy and great improvements in hull and sail plan were coming rapidly. Above water, hulls lost the topheavy fore and after erections and the masses of decorations began to disappear until only a figure or billethead, trailboards and a light stern ornament remained. Below water, lines became finer and longer. Sail areas necessarily were enlarged usually by increasing the heights of the masts and adding sails rather than by enlarging the proportion of width. Square head-sails disappeared to be replaced by the more efficient jibs, and staysails changed their shapes from trapezoids to triangles. Sails themselves were made of cotton duck instead of linen. Rigging was lighter yet stronger and much iron work was now to be found about the hull and spars. After 1780 sheets of copper covered the bottoms replacing the ineffective mixtures of tallow, brimstone, and vertigris as protection against worms and barnacles. By 1807 Captain John Smith would have found so many changes he would have needed a guide and could not have qualified as a seaman.

The remaining days of sail saw only minor changes: the size of vessels increased substantially; more and more, metals replaced wood; wire rigging took the place of hemp in many pieces of gear; there were roller bearings in blocks; and topsails were divided for easier handling. Even the rigs of the Bay's deep-sea traders were changed from the traditional ship and bark to the barkentine in the flour-coffee trade and to the three and four masted schooner rig in the Coastal and West-India trades. The last large square rigged vessel was the *Baltimore* built for the coffee trade at Baltimore in 1889; the last brig, the whaler *Alexander,* built at Cambridge in 1886 for the Behring Sea whale fishery; the last big schooner the *Lillian E. Kerr* built at Pocomoke City in 1920.

A Seventeenth Century ketch typical of those used in the colonial trade about 1670. Water color in The British Museum.

A merchant ship of the type used in the tobacco trade about 1670. Water color in The British Museum.

An early Eighteenth Century galley-built merchant ship. Note the ports for oars used in calm weather. Drawing from The Hakluyt Society.

A typical Mid-Eighteenth Century merchant ship in the colonial trade. Water color in The M. H. de Young Museum.

The ship *Harriet* of Georgetown off the Dutch coast. Engraving by G. Groenewegen, 1793, owned by The Naval Historical Foundation.

Ship *Jane* of Baltimore off Den Helder, 1830, flying house flag of William Wilson and showing his black main upper sail. Water color at The Maryland Historical Society.

Ship *Eliza Ann* of Salem, built in Baltimore, 1835. Water color in The Peabody Museum, Salem.

Duplicate of the Bills
Presented Lengths and Sizes of the

Spars made for the Ship Ann M. Nash(?)

Fore mast	63	23	1449
main mast	70	24	1680
mizen mast	60	17	1020
fore top mast	40	15	600
main top mast	41	15	615
mizen top mast	31	12	372
fore yd	47	12	564
main Do	55	14	770
mizen Do	42	10½	441
Jib Boom	42	13½	367
Bow Sprit	35	24	840
fore topsail yd	34	9½	323
main Do Do Do	44	11	
mizen Do Do Do			244
fore T. G. yd	25		133
main T. G. yd	33		247
mizen T. G. yd	20	5	100
fore royal yd	19	4	76
main Do Do	26	5¼	136½
mizen Do Do	13	3¼	42½
main tob Ga'lant mast	41	8¼	372
fore Do Do Do	49	9	361
mizen Do Do Do	31	7	217
Spanker Boom	38	8½	323
Swinging Booms	40	7¼	580
fore topsail mast	35	6½	292½
main Do	40	9	360
mizen Do	27	6½	175½
			13425

"Length and Sizes of the Spars made for the ship *Ann McKim.*" Account books of Kennard & Williamson, shipbuilders of Baltimore, 1833, owned by The Maryland Historical Society.

	feet long	inches diameter
Foremast	63	23
Mainmast	70	24
Misenmast	60	17
fore Topmast	40	15
main topmast	41	15
Misen topmast	31	12
fore yd	47	12
Main do	55	14
Misen do	42	10½
Gib Boom	42	13½
Bowsprit	35	24
fore Top Sail yd	36	9½
main do do do	44	11½
Misen do do do	30	8
fore T G yd	25	5½
main T G yd	33	7½
misen T G yd	20	5
fore royal yd	18	4
main Do Do	26	5½
Misen Do Do	13	3¼

	feet long	inches diameter
main top Gallant mast	41	9¼
fore Do Do Do	39	9
Misen Do Do Do	31	7
Spanker Boom	38	8½
Swinging Booms	40	7¼
fore tri Sail mast	35	8½
main Do	46	9
Misen Do	27	6½
fore Gaff	24	7
main Do	25	7
Misen Do	28	6½
2 Fore topmast Steering Sail Booms	26	7
2 main do do	30	7
2 fore Top G. Steering Sail Booms	20	5
main do do	24½	6
2 Steering Sail yd	19	4½
2 Do Do Do	15	4
2 Do Do Do	16	4
1 Do Do Do	18	4½
1 Do Do Do	13	3¼

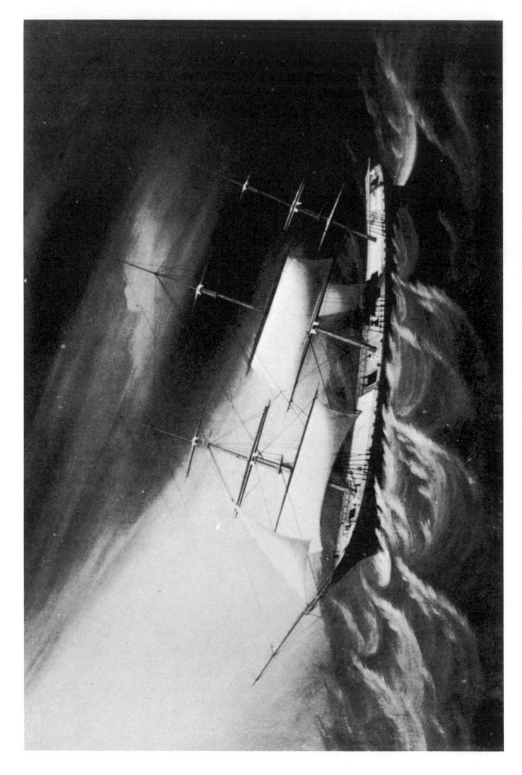

Clipper ship *Mary Whitridge*, built in Baltimore, 1855, by Hunt and Wagner. Photograph owned by The Maryland Historical Society.

Clipper ship *Seaman's Bride,* built in Baltimore, 1851, by E. J. and R. Bell. Oil painting owned by The Maryland Historical Society.

Full-built ship *Eliza,* built in Baltimore, 1856. Oil painting by A. H. Buttersworth owned by The Mariners' Museum.

Brig *Cruger* of Salem, built in Maryland, 1788. Water color owned by The Peabody Museum, Salem.

Brig *Harriet* of Baltimore, 1823. Water color by Montardier of Havre, owned by The Maryland Historical Society.

Brig *Golden Age* (?) of Norfolk. Oil painting by unidentified Chinese artist, owned by The Mariners' Museum.

Hermaphrodite brig *Northumberland*, built in Baltimore, 1839. Either a slaver or African trader as she is armed and has boarding nets rigged. Oil painting by unidentified artist, owned by The Peabody Museum, Salem.

Brigantine *Garland* of Salem, built at Baltimore, 1847. Oil painting owned by The Peabody Museum, Salem.

Brigantine *Zaine* of Salem, built at Church Creek, Dorchester County, Maryland, by Aaron and Jesse Richardson, 1840. Oil painting by unidentified artist, owned by The Peabody Museum, Salem.

Bark *General Stricker*, built in Baltimore, 1857, for the Rio coffee trade. Oil painting owned by
The Maryland Historical Society.

Barkentine *Josephine II*, built at Belfast, Maine, 1896, for the Rio coffee trade. She set
all-time record Rio-Baltimore in 1897, 24 days 13 hours wharf to wharf. Oil painting owned by
C. Morton Stewart.

Schooner *Federal George* of Baltimore, built at Duxbury, Mass., 1794. Water color owned by the Peabody Museum, Salem.

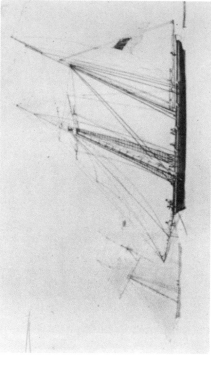

Baltimore clipper schooners. Acquatint by W. J. Huggins, ca. 1825, owned by The National Maritime Museum.

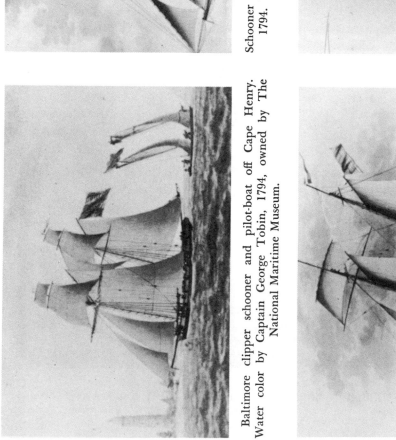

Baltimore clipper schooner and pilot-boat off Cape Henry. Water color by Captain George Tobin, 1794, owned by The National Maritime Museum.

Baltimore clipper schooner reefed down. Lithograph by J. Rogers, 1825, owned by The National Maritime Museum.

Schooner *H. H. Cole* of Salem, built in Baltimore, 1843. Oil painting by C. Drew owned by The Peabody Museum, Salem.

Four masted schooner *Purnell T. White*, built at Sharptown, Maryland, by Alonzo Conoly, 1917. Oil painting by Antonio Jacobsen owned by The Maryland Historical Society.

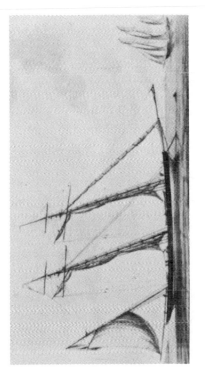

Three masted Baltimore clipper schooner anchored off Cape Henry. Lithograph by J. Rogers, 1825, owned by The National Maritime Museum.

Schooner *Anandale* towing through railroad bridge at Vienna on the way to sea.

Deck view, *Anandale*, looking forward. Photographs owned by H. Robins Hollyday.

Schooner *Anandale*, built at Sharptown, Maryland, 1919, the last large sailing vessel built on Chesapeake Bay.

Deck view, *Anandale*, looking aft.

IV.

Steamboats

LATE in the Eighteenth Century passenger traffic through the Atlantic Coastal States increased greatly. Most of it was transported by horse drawn coaches over bad roads, although usually wherever a body of water ran in the right direction a change to watercraft was made. One of the principal links in the chain lay between Baltimore and Philadelphia. From the latter the traveller went by boat down the Delaware River to New Castle or Wilmington, then transferred to a coach which carried him a few miles to the Elk River where another change was made to a boat which carried him to Baltimore. Should he be bound further South a third boat took him down the Chesapeake to Norfolk. By 1812 there were four lines of daily sailing vessels (schooners and sloops) running between Baltimore and the Elk, two lines between Baltimore and Norfolk; and a half dozen from Baltimore and Norfolk to the smaller Bay and river towns. All the packet lines advertised their vessels to be "fast sailing" but none of them attempted to foretell an arrival time: wind and tide, not man, ruled that.

On both the Delaware and the waters around New York the commercial and engineering practicality of steam propelled vessels had been demonstrated by 1810 and after an investigation of those steamboat operations, the Union Line of Baltimore led by Captain Edward Trippe decided to try a steamer on the Bay. This was the *Chesapeake*, built by William Flanigan of Baltimore. After two exhibition trips, on 21 June 1813 she began regular runs to Frenchtown on the Elk. The venture was immediately successful, almost driving the competing sailing packet lines out of business. One, The Briscoe & Partridge Line, chartered the steamboat *Eagle* in July 1815, whereupon the Union Line built a second steamer the *Baltimore*. Steamer service on the Potomac was commenced the same year with the *Washington*. The following year a Norfolk-Baltimore packet operator, Benjamin Ferguson, built the steamboat *Virginia* for his line which connected with the steamboat *Powhatan* running from Norfolk to Richmond.

From then on the history of the steamboat on the Chesapeake was one of steady expansion of the routes by small companies until every Bay or river port had both freight and passenger service to Baltimore, Washington, or Norfolk. The Civil War disrupted most of the services because the Federal government pressed many of the steamboats for military purposes, but at the end of the war, the services were restored and competition on some of the routes became strenuous. Rate wars began and before long the weaker lines were forced into mergers. By 1900 three large companies controlled practically all the services. These virtual monopolies, however, did not lead to a public-be-damned attitude since almost everyone who used the boats knew every member of the crews from captain to coal passer and with such personal accountability at stake the service and food left little to be desired. Faster and more comfortable boats were added steadily until shortly before World War I. After the war competition from motor cars and trucks began to be serious and a rapid decline in both passenger and freight traffic set in. By the middle Twenties the principal operator, the Baltimore, Chesapeake and Atlantic Railroad, was curtailing some of its routes and within a few years all the steamboats except those of the Old Bay Line were gone. That company, now the oldest line in the country, still maintains the service started in 1817.

One unique type of steamboat exists on a Bay tributary, one designed not for passengers or handling freight but for one specific job—recovering submerged coal. Since its earliest days the Susquehanna River has been flowing over rich coal seams, eroding them and carrying fragments down stream. On shore in later days coal mines in washing their produce have been sending more coal into the river. Busy recovering this lost coal is a sizeable fleet of steamboats whose appearance must make a naval architect shudder: a scow hull on which is mounted a horizontal boiler and engine like those of an old fashioned wheat threshing rig. Coupled to the engine by belts are a stern paddle wheel and a centrifugal pump. The stern wheel propels the boat over a coal bar; the pump brings the submerged coal onto the boat, and after supplying its own boiler, the remainder of the catch is sold.

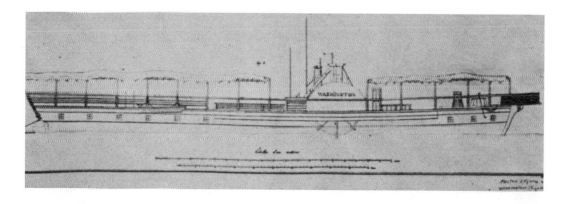

Steamboat *Washington*, built at New York, 1815, for service on the Potomac River. Engraved plan from M. Marestier: *Mèmoire sur les Bateaux à Vapeur . . . des Etats Unis,* 1824.

Steamboat *Pocahontas*, built at Baltimore, by Beacham & Gardner, 1829, for the Elk River-Baltimore route, later Old Bay Line. Drawing owned by The National Maritime Museum.

Steamboat *Tred Avon,* built by W. E. Woodall & Co., Baltimore, 1884, for the Choptank Steamboat Co., on the Easton run. Photograph owned by H. Graham Wood.

Steamboat *Westmoreland,* built by William Skinner & Sons, at Baltimore, 1883, for the Weems Line to the Patuxent and Rappahannock Rivers. Photograph owned by H. Graham Wood.

Steamboat *Emma Giles,* built by W. E. Woodall & Co., at Baltimore, 1887 for the Tolchester Line to Annapolis and Little Choptank River. Photograph owned by H. Osborne Michael.

Steamboat *Tangier,* built by Harlan & Hollingsworth, at Wilmington, Delaware, 1875, for the Eastern Shore Steamboat Co., on the Pocomoke and Crisfield runs. Photograph owned by H. Graham Wood.

Steamboat *Cambridge,* built by W. E. Woodall & Co., at Baltimore, 1890, said to be the fastest River steamboat on the Bay. Photograph owned by H. Graham Wood

Steamboat *Kent* built at Baltimore, 1854. Photograph owned by H. Graham Wood.

Steamboat *Enoch Pratt,* built at Baltimore, 1878, for the Maryland Steamboat Co. to Piankatank River. Photograph owned by H. Graham Wood.

Steamboat *Choptank*, built by Thomas McCosker & Co. at Baltimore, 1883, for the Choptank Steamboat Co. Photograph owned by H. Graham Wood.

Steamboat *Joppa,* built by Harlan & Hollingsworth, at Wilmington, Delaware, 1885, for the Maryland Steamboat Co. for Choptank River run. Photograph owned by H. Graham Wood.

Steamboats *Dorchester* and *Talbot,* built by Maryland Steel Co., Baltimore, 1912, for the Baltimore, Chesapeake and Atlantic Railroad Co., for Choptank River service; Steamboat *Virginia,* built by Maryland Steel Co., at Baltimore, 1903, for Wicomico River service—tied up at Baltimore, 1935, their passenger days on the Bay ended. Photograph by Robert H. Burgess.

Steamboat *Pocahontas*, built at Wilmington, Delaware, 1893, for the James River service. Lithograph owned by The Mariners' Museum.

Steamboat *Virginia*, built by Harlan & Hollingsworth, at Wilmington, Delaware, 1905, for the Old Bay Line. Lithograph owned by The Mariner's Museum.

Steamboat *State of Maryland,* built by Pusey & Jones, at Wilmington, Delaware, 1922, for the Old Bay Line. Oil Painting by Bishop, owned by The Mariners' Museum.

Steamboat *City of Norfolk,* built by Maryland Steel Co., at Baltimore, 1911, for the Chesapeake Steamboat Co., now the Old Bay Line. Photograph by Robert H. Burgess.

Baltimore Harbor at the height of steamboat days ninety-nine years after the introduction of the steamboat on the Bay. L. to R. *City of Norfolk, Atlanta, Susquehanna, Florida, Gaston, Elsie, Piankatank, Cambridge, Westmoreland, Old Point Comfort, Avalon, Anne Arundel, Calvert, Three Rivers, Middlesex, Anthony Groves, Jr., Maryland* or *Virginia, Eastern Shore, Tivoli, Annapolis.* Photograph by J. H. Schaefer & Son, 1912.

Steamboat wharf at Nanticoke, Maryland, 1918. Photograph by William Willing.

Steamboat wharf at Secretary, Maryland, 1904. Photograph by Raymond Spears.

Steamboat wharf on Mobjack Bay, Virginia, 1904. Photograph by Raymond Spears.

Steamship *William Lawrence,* built by The Atlantic Works, East Boston, Mass., 1868, for The Merchants & Miners Line. Lithograph owned by The Mariners' Museum.

Steamship *Ontario,* built by The New York Shipbuilding Co., Camden, N. J., 1904, for The Merchants & Miners Line. Lithograph owned by The Mariners' Museum.

Coal recovery steamboat on the Susquehanna River. Photograph by A. C. Brown, 1949.

V.

Ferries

THE FIRST public utility in the New World was the ferry boat. Almost simultaneously in 1638 Virginia and Maryland provided the means whereby their citizens could cross rivers to reach their principal settlements from outlying plantations. Maryland's ferry was established by the provincial legislature to enable the burgesses to get to St. Mary's City; Virginia's came by way of court sentence: one John for committing fornication was ordered to set up a ferry over Old Plantation Creek or take thirty lashes with the whip. From 1638 onward nearly to the present no form of water transport—the Western Ocean packets, the clippers, or the emigrant steamers—did as much for as many persons as the ubiquitous river ferry. By 1758 Virginia had 138 operating with official sanction and Maryland as many more. Every river had at least one and some, the Potomac for instance, a dozen. Many are still operating: in Wicomico County, Maryland, there are four working in the Eighteenth Century manner, a flat boat about forty-five feet long with one man by the strength of his arms and back pulling the boat across the stream along a rope stretched from bank to bank.

Earliest of these ferries were log canoes which were poled or paddled across the stream. When wagons put in appearance, two canoes were lashed together with the right wheels of the vehicle resting in one canoe, the left wheels in the other canoe and the horses swimming. Flats or broad-beamed row boats which could take the team and vehicle aboard followed. For long distance trips over the Bay from the Eastern to the Western Shore, sailing vessels, fast sloops or schooners, with sleeping accommodations in case of foul winds, and space on deck for horses and vehicles were used. George Washington on one trip from Rock Hall on the Eastern Shore to Annapolis on the Western needed fourteen hours for his passage, experiencing calms, two squalls, grounding, and rescue by a small boat. His horses which had been embarked at the same time in another boat had crossed in five hours. Usually the same trip was made in four hours in perfect comfort. In the Mid-Eighteenth Century three ferry routes crossed the Bay from Annapolis to the Eastern Shore and other routes ran from the end of the peninsula to Norfolk, Yorktown, and Hampton.

In 1853 the ferry-packets from the Eastern Shore of Virginia to Norfolk were replaced by the steamboat *Joseph E. Coffee* running four days each week. Those crossing the upper Bay seem to have been put out of business by the net work of steamboat services from the Eastern Shore to Baltimore which had superceded Annapolis in all save politics. The rapid increase in motor traffic brought a demand again for cross Bay ferries from Cape to Cape and from the Eastern Shore to the Western. At first more or less antiquated steamers and ancient harbor ferries, limited in capacity to a few cars, were put in service. The Claiborne-Annapolis, later Matapeake-Sandy Point, ferry began operation in 1919; the Virginia Ferry Corporation, Cape Charles-Little Creek, in 1931. As traffic continued to mount, many especially designed streamlined diesel craft took over the cross-Bay and the more important river crossings. Even these could not properly serve the public, and stream after stream has been bridged. Finally in 1952 the Bay was spanned by a great bridge which brought the era of enforced use of watercraft on the Chesapeake to an end.

Yet with all the bridge and submarine tunnel building at both ends of the Bay, the Commonwealth of Virginia in 1955 has organized an authority to operate ferries across the Bay from the Eastern Shore to some point in the Tidewater Country not directly approached by the existing routes.

Row ferry over York River, Virginia. Photograph from A. C. Brown.

Sailing ferries and packets at Turkey Point, Elk River, Maryland. Pencil drawing by J. H. B. Latrobe in F. Lucas, Jr.: *Progressive Drawing Book.*

Rope ferry over Wicomico River, below Salisbury, Maryland, 1940. Photograph by M. V. Brewington.

Annapolis-Claiborne ferry *Majestic*, 1925. Photograph by H. Robins Hollyday.

Sandy Point-Matapeake ferry *Gov. Herbert R. O'Conor,* 1952.
Photograph by H. Robins Hollyday.

Cape Charles-Little Creek ferry *Princess Anne,* 1951. Photograph from The Virginia Ferry
Corporation.

Chesapeake Bay Bridge, 1952, looking east. Sandy Point ferry slip, left foreground. Photograph from W. Avery Hall and State Roads Commission.

VI.

Baycraft

AFTER 1590 when the drawings John White had made at Ralegh's Roanoke settlement were published, Englishmen were familiar with the dugout canoes the southern Indians built. The colonists at Jamestown were quick to adopt these canoes, so great was their need for watercraft which could not otherwise be obtained. The white man's superior knowledge of small craft soon indicated changes which would improve the canoe: sharp ends would make her easier to propel and more seaworthy; broader beam and a keel would increase stability; sail would lessen the work of getting from place to place. Sharpening the bow and stern was a simple matter: the increased beam was difficult because no single tree could provide the needed width. In time the settler learned how to join two or more trees together to give the beam desired. He learned how to add topsides, first of hewn logs, later of sawed plank. A keel was added and a sailing rig. After the centerboard was invented, it took the place of a keel. Three variations of hull and rig eventually developed from the basic design, one in Virginia, the Poquoson canoe; and two on the Eastern Shore, the Pocomoke and the Tilghman's Island canoes.

But the culmination of the simple, single log, trough-shaped Indian dugout was the bugeye, a complex vessel as much as eighty-five feet in length. There was an intermediate step between the canoe and the bugeye, the brogan, a large canoe, partially decked, with a cuddy forward in which a couple of men could sleep and cook. Its rig was that of a Tilghman's Island canoe. The earliest known use of the name bugeye is in 1868, but like the word schooner it doubtless was not coined upon the first appearance of the vessel itself. However all evidence points to the development of the bugeye immediately after the Civil War, soon after the legalization of the heavy iron dredge which required a more powerful vessel than a canoe or brogan to pull it over the oyster beds. Of course schooners, pungies, and sloops could be used but they were costly to build or buy and not specifically adapted to the trade as was the bugeye. In essence the bugeye was a large canoe, fully decked, with a fixed rig following that of the brogan. There were full accommodations for the crew which because the vessel was built for oyster dredging needed to be comparatively large, since in addition to sailing, steering, and cooking, the oyster dredges with their winders had to be handled and the catch stowed. Throughout the course of development from canoe to bugeye the original dugout log bottom was always apparent in this most truly American craft. Eventually logs became difficult to obtain in large sizes and too costly since so much of the log was wasted and bugeyes began to be built by conventional frame and plank methods.

In contrast with the American origin of the bugeye, the sloop, perhaps by way of the shallop, came directly from Europe both hull and rig. The name itself was in use of the Bay in 1648. Originally it seems to have been rigged with a square-headed spritsail and a fore staysail and sometime later exchanged the sprit for a gaff. The earliest known picture of a Bay sloop, that on the plat of Oxford in 1707, conforms exactly with those shown in contemporary Dutch and English pictures. The captain of the only sloop afloat today would easily recognize his rig in the Oxford sloop of two and a half centuries ago, and would have no difficulty handling her.

What the true origin of the schooner may have been has not yet been traced. By 1713 the name was in use in New England. Written records of Bay shipping are not plentiful in the early Eighteenth Century, hence the first discovered use there may be late: it comes in 1716 with a mention of the schooner *Mayflower* of North Carolina arriving in the Bay. The next year the "skooner" *Marlboro* of Boston came through the Capes followed by the schooner *George* of Jamaica. The widespread homes of these three, Boston, North Carolina, and Jamaica (and it is known there were others at New York and Philadelphia) within five years after the "invention" at Gloucester in 1713 shows clearly how quickly the rig had been accepted by coastal vessels. Within a score of years the first specialized schooner the Virginia pilot-boat was well known. From it developed the Baltimore Clipper as a deep-sea craft and the pungy as a Bay craft. To the end of their days both remained keel vessels with curved raking stems, sharp bows, long fine runs, deep drag aft, square stern with straight raking posts, low bulwarks (log rail on most pungies) with sail plans sharply raked, lofty and narrow. Not all the schooner rigged vessels on the Bay were built for speed—there was little need for it in many trades and cargo capacity more important. Until the invention of the centerboard they were keel craft but without the fine deep lines of the pungy and with a lower, broader sail plan. To distinguish them from the pungy, the burdensome craft seem to have been known as clump-schooners and when the centerboard was applied to them, simply as a schooner. Another adaptation of the schooner on the Bay was called a ram. Like all such names, pungy, clump, bugeye, ram is obscure in origin. The vessel was developed primarily for trading through the Chesapeake and Delaware Canal with beam and draft to fit the lock chambers. It was a straight, wall-sided vessel with very full ends, much like a canal boat, but it was given a centerboard and a bald-head (i.e., without topmasts) schooner rig. In later days most of them were three masted, the great majority built on the Nanticoke River across the State line in Delaware. Another type of hull given the schooner rig was the scow. This, too, was a specialized development brought about by a local condition. In use as early as 1743 it carried pig iron from the furnaces at the Head of the Bay down to the foreign traders anchored in deep water. The hull was that of the common scow: square sided, usually without change in beam from the square raked bow to an identical stern. Hatches filled most of the deck. After the iron was exhausted their use continued around Havre de Grace until the 1940's, but in later years the scows generally carried a sloop, instead of a schooner, rig.

The last type of sailing craft to be developed on the Bay was the skipjack, in some localities called a batteau, in others, a dead rise. Its was a design caused not by hydrographic but by economic conditions: the depressed period in business in the early 1890's, and the decline in oyster production at the same time. Just as the bugeye had the canoe as its parent, the skipjack was sired by the V-bottom skiff commonly used in sailing along the crab trot lines in the shoal waters of the lower Eastern Shore. Almost any waterman could and did build small skipjacks. They were simple in design, required no special tools or much hardware, rigging, and equipment; hence they were cheap to construct when compared with other vessels. Furthermore they were cheap to operate—one man could handle one with ease and in a pinch even take care of the dredge as well in mild weather. The first boats, those of the 1890's were small and stayed near home, selling their catch to buy boats from the cities or to local oyster houses. By 1901, the skipjacks had grown large enough to carry their catch to Baltimore, and one marine reporter commented in that year about the "new" type of vessel then appearing in the harbor. Another few years saw them reach their peak in size with the building of the *Robert L. Webster* by Sylvester Muir at Oriole, Maryland, in 1915. She was sixty feet on deck. All the larger vessels were built by professional shipbuilders. The skipjack is the only Bay sailing craft of size which has been built since 1918.

The skiff on the Bay has had at least fourteen designs, each differing somewhat from the others. All but two are commonly called batteau locally, sharing the name in a few places with the skipjack. The exceptions are the cabin skiff (pronounced "skift") of Talbot County and the gilling skiff of the extreme upper Bay. Of the batteaus, some are double-enders; some have square sterns; some are flat-bottomed; some full V-bottomed and some between. One, the gilling skiff is round bottomed. Some have cross planked bottoms; some herring bone; some are fore-and-aft planked on frames. Some are partially decked with a cuddy forward, others are open except for wash boards. Most of them are built by the watermen themselves, each man acting as his own designer and only at Smith's and Holland's Island was there a local type: square stern, fore-and-aft planked full V-bottom. Like most homemade humble things the article itself is the only record of its existence, in the case of a boat, a very fugitive sort of record. It is known that there was a "skiffe" in Virginia as early as 1624, and the word is found frequently thereafter, but what they were is not known. Aside from an occasional newspaper ad for a lost boat, usually obscurely worded, nothing is to be found until the United States Fish Commission began to notice the various types of watercraft used in the fisheries. The Commission's descriptions carrying the record back to the 1880's include only those we knew through the remaining skiffs.

Practically all the skiffs were used for crabbing or tonging, the one exception being the gilling skiff found in the shad fishery in the upper Bay. These boats originated in the Delaware River shad and sturgeon fisheries and came to the Bay by way of the Chesapeake and Delaware Canal. Those built on the Bay were always the work of professional builders, only four of whom can be traced in Maryland. Another skiff type used around the Bay was the Staten Island skiff, one of which is the row ferry depicted in Chapter V. Here is one type whose origin in the Bay can be definitely fixed. The boats were all built on Staten Island, N. Y. and brought to the lower Bay, particularly to the York River by the Van Name family who were New

York dealers owning large oyster beds in the Virginia Rivers. Native to the Bay but very different from all other skiff types was the cabin skiff of Talbot County. At a short distance it could easily be mistaken for a brogan since it was a double-ender, half decked with a cuddy forward and a two masted canoe rig. But there the similarity ended for the sides were of plank bent around a full V-bottom made of very heavy sawed lumber running fore-and-aft, the pieces edge-bolted together. No commercial sailing skiffs are being used today: the second-hand auto engine has driven them all out of existence.

Not all design ingenuity passed with sail: when internal combustion engines first appeared about 1904 they offered a challenge the Bay builders quickly accepted. The earliest of the motor boats seem to have been canoes shorn of rig and centerboard. They were successful but overly heavy and slow. Next a miniature of the typical tugboat hull complete with fan-tail stern was tried; that also proved to be too expensive. Then came a V-bottom hull with a rounded stern like that of the back end of a Chippendale claw foot bath tub. It was cheaper though the stern settled so badly when underway "squatboards" were necessary. One builder who lived in a place where every vessel bound up the Bay almost had to pass his door, frequently saw torpedo boat destroyers race by. Thinking such a hull would make a good motor boat, what he could see of their hulls above water he copied from stem to stern. With a V-bottom she gave the Baymen everything they wanted, speed, low cost, and beauty. Named the Hooper's Island boat after the home of the first builder, the design spread all over the Bay in a short time. Unfortunately when the stock cabin cruiser tricked out with chrome and bright trim became commonplace, the Hooper's Island boats looked old fashioned and the watermen demanded the newer type. Today the Hooper's Island boat, rapidly disappearing and no longer being built, has even lost its name and is called a duck-tail. The new boats, broad beamed, high sided, square sterned affairs are given the name "box stern"—a very apt description.

Indian canoe builders at work, 1585. From a drawing by John White in Hariot: *Virginia*.

Rev. Joshua Thomas' canoe *Methodist*. From Adam Wallace: *The Parson of the Islands,* 1872.

Tilghman's Island canoe *Mary Rider*. Oil painting by Louis Feuchter, 1948, owned by The Mariners' Museum.

Pocomoke canoe with stick-up jib. Photograph from Colgate Hoyt.

Poquoson canoe under construction, York County, Virginia, 1935, by Clyde Smith.

Bottom being shaped.

Interior rough-hollowed, sides being built up.

Bare hull completed.

Interior of finished canoe, looking aft.   Interior of finished canoe, looking forward.

Ready to launch. Photographs owned by The Mariners' Museum.

Tonging canoes at St. Michaels about 1900. Photograph owned by John G. Earle.

On the way to town. Pocomoke type canoe with stick-up jib on the Wicomico River, 1904. Photograph by Raymond Spears.

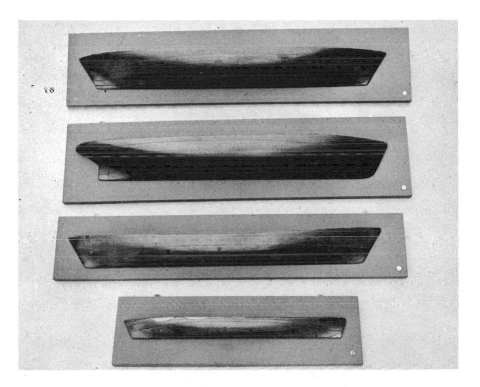

Builder's half models of Bay craft. Top to bottom: frame bugeye, round-stern bugeye, log bugeye, log canoe.

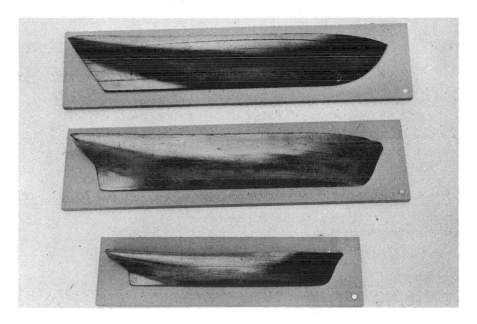

Pungy, schooner, sloop. All from the collection of M. V. Brewington.

Builders' half models of Bay craft. Top to bottom: gilling skiff, two skipjacks, four crab skiffs. All from the collection of M. V. Brewington.

Brogans tonging. Photograph by George Barrie, Jr., about 1902.

Brogan underway. Photograph by George Barrie, Jr., about 1902.

Interior of frame bugeye *Nora Phillips* under construction by James Marsh, Solomon's Island, Maryland, 1901. Photograph by George Barrie, Jr.

Exterior of frame bugeye *Nora Phillips*. Photograph by George Barrie, Jr.

Round-stern bugeye *Emma A. Faulkner,* becalmed off St. Michaels, Maryland, 1921. Photograph by C. Lowndes Johnson.

Round-stern bugeye *Norma,* built by Otis Lloyd, Salisbury, Maryland, 1901. Photograph by Otis Lloyd.

Bugeye *Brown Smith Jones,* Maryland Oyster Navy, built by George T. Johnson, Cambridge, Maryland, 1894. Photograph from Linton Rigg.

Bugeye *Little Jennie,* off Oxford, Maryland. Photograph by H. Robins Hollyday.

Bugeye *Clarence & Eva*, dredging oysters off Rock Hall, Maryland. Photograph by Frank A. Moorshead, Jr.

Bugeye *Lizzie J. Cox*. Oil painting by Louis Feuchter, 1947, owned by The Mariners' Museum.

Bugeyes fitting out on the first railway at Salisbury ca. 1880. Photograph owned by James Perry.

Main mast of bugeye.

Fore mast head of bugeye.

Patent stern of bugeye.

Jib sheet of bugeye.

Foresail sheet of
bugeye.

Mainsail sheet of
bugeye. All pho-
tographs by M. V.
Brewington.

Bow of bugeye *Lizzie J. Cox;* stern of bugeye *Florence,* Cambridge Creek, Maryland, 1932.
Photograph by M. V. Brewington.

Round-stern bugeye, *G. W. Glenn,* on railway at Salisbury, Maryland, 1932. Photograph
by M. V. Brewington.

Launch of round-stern bugeye *Margaret A. Travers,* Salisbury, Maryland, 1901. Photograph by Otis Lloyd.

"Square-rigged" bugeye *George T. Phillips,* Miles River, Maryland, 1915. Photograph by C. Lowndes Johnson.

Sloop *J. T. Leonard*, built by Moses Geoghegan, Taylor's Island, Maryland, 1882. Oil painting by Louis Feuchter, 1949, owned by The Mariners' Museum.

Mast head, sloop *J. T. Leonard*, 1939. Photograph by M. V. Brewington.

Sloop *William Wesley,* built at Crisfield, Maryland, 1874. Photographs by C. Lowndes Johnson.

Scow sloop *Elsie,* built Philadelphia, 1874, rebuilt Havre de Grace, 1890. Photograph by H. Osborne Michael.

Scow sloop *Elsie* at work boat races. Photograph by C. Lowndes Johnson.

Details of scow sloop *Elsie* in 1940. Photographs by Frank A. Moorshead, Jr.

Pungy *James A. Whiting,* built Somerset County, Maryland, 1871. Oil painting by Louis Feuchter, 1947, owned by The Mariners' Museum.

Pungy *James A. Whiting,* unloading lumber at Baltimore, Maryland. Photograph by W. C. Steuart.

Pungy *Amanda F. Lewis,* built by Joseph W. Brooks, Madison, Maryland, 1884, anchored in the Coan River, Virginia. Photograph by W. C. Steuart.

Pungy *Francis J. Ruth,* built Dorchester County, Maryland, 1871, loaded with railroad ties. Photograph by C. Lowndes Johnson.

Pungy *Lucy J. Stewart,* built Somerset County, Maryland, 1869. Photograph by Frank A. Moorshead.

Pungy *Wave*, built in Accomac County, Virginia, 1863, at Crosby, Maryland, 1937. Photograph by A. C. Brown.

Pungy *Wave,* bow.

Pungy *Wave,* windlass.

Pungy *Wave,* deck looking
aft.

Pungy *Wave*, quarter trunk and cabin.

Pungy *Wave*, wheel and transom. Photographs by M. V. Brewington.

Pungy *Wave*, interior of cabin, bulkhead torn out. Photograph by John G. Earle.

Pungy *Wave,* main mast head.

Pungy *Wave,* hold looking aft.

Pungy *Wave,* hold looking forward. Photographs by M. V. Brewington.

Schooner *William H. Michael*, built in Queen Anne County, Maryland, 1879.
Photograph by H. Osborne Michael.

Schooner *Mattie F. Dean*, built by Joseph W. Brooks, Madison, Maryland, 1884. Oil painting by Louis Feuchter, 1948, owned by The Mariners' Museum.

Schooner *Annie C. Johnson,* built by M. M. Davis, at Solomon's Island, Maryland, 1891. Photograph by M. V. Brewington.

Schooner *Frank and Theresa*, built at Leesburg, N. J., 1900, in Miles River, Maryland. Photograph by C. Lowndes Johnson.

Schooner *Eddie Cook*, built at Cambridge, Maryland, 1883. Photograph by Richard Goldsborough.

Schooner *Minnie May Kirwan*, built by Steven Murrell, at White Haven, Maryland, 1882. Photograph by Frank A. Moorshead, Jr., 1938.

Schooner *Maine*, of Washington, D. C., built by the New England Shipbuilding Co., at Bath, Maine, 1886. Note differences in hull and rig from Bay type schooner. Photograph by Frank A. Moorshead, Jr.

Schooner *Edward V. Hendrickson* of Denton passing through Dover Bridge, Choptank River, Maryland. Photograph by H. Robbins Hollyday.

Ram *Edwin & Maud,* built by J. M. C. Moore, at Bethel, Delaware, 1900. Oil painting by Louis Feuchter, 1948, owned by The Mariners' Museum.

Ram *William J. Stanford,* ex *John B. Conner,* built at Barker's Landing, Delaware, 1868. Photograph by Frank A. Moorshead, Jr., 1938.

Skipjack dredging oysters, 1938. Photograph by Frank A. Moorshead, Jr.

Skipjack *Jesse Price,* built at Oriole, Maryland, 1908. Oil painting by Louis Feuchter, 1948, owned by The Mariners' Museum.

Skipjack *Gladys,* built by Oliver Duke, Royal Oak, Maryland, 1896.
Photograph by Richard Goldsborough.

Skipjack *Annie Bennett,* built by John Branford, Fishing Island, Maryland,
1898, ready to be launched. Photograph owned by M. V. Brewington.

Skipjacks laid up for summer, Chance, Maryland, 1940. Photograph by M. V. Brewington.

Skipjack *Mary E.*, built at Hopkins, Virginia, 1901, blocked up for painting, Wenona, Maryland, 1938. Photograph by M. V. Brewington.

Two masted skipjack *Virgie G. Dean,* built at Bishop's Head, Maryland, 1897. Photograph by Raymond Spears, 1904.

Skipjack at season's end and a double-ended crab skiff, Deal's Island, Maryland, 1936. Photograph by M. V. Brewington.

Skipjack using water-sail or "save-all". Photograph by Frank A. Moorshead, 1918.

Three skipjacks under construction 1955, by B. M. Parks, Wingate, Maryland. Photograph by Emory Stafford.

Hand scraping for crabs, Wenona, Maryland, 1938. Photograph by M. V. Brewington.

Sunday rest. Skipjacks in Cambridge Creek, Maryland, 1950. Photograph by Clinton De Witt.

Crab skiffs. Oil painting by Louis Feuchter, 1949, owned by The Mariners' Museum.

Large crab skiff, built by John Branford, Fishing Island, Maryland, 1918. Photograph by M. V. Brewington.

Typical Smith's Island crab skiff at Wenona, Maryland, 1935. Crab shedding floats are to be seen inside the breakwater fence. Photograph by M. V. Brewington.

Gilling skiff out for a Sunday sail, about 1902. Cabin skiff *Doctor Johnson*, about 1900. Photo-
Photograph by H. Osborne Michael.　　　　graph by C. Lowndes Johnson.

Sharpies tied up at Ocean City, Maryland, 1932. Photograph by M. V. Brewington.

Crab skiff, stern construction, Deal's Island, Maryland, 1940. Photograph by M. V. Brewington.

Crab skiff, bow construction, interior. Photograph by John G. Earle.

Crab skiff, bow construction, exterior. Photograph by M. V. Brewington.

VII.

The Ports

ARLY views of Bay ports and harbors are virtually non-existent for the very simple reason that there were few ports in the usual sense and these in the early years had more political than commercial significance. Because port towns would aid in collecting duties if all tobacco had to pass through them, legislative attempts to create them were numerous and usually unsuccessful. In 1694, for instance, one law established nearly a score of towns on various parts of Maryland's waterfront. Few survived: there was no economic need for most, and those which did owed their lives to some English merchant who opened a factory, or branch, of his London, Bristol, or Liverpool establishment in the town. There small planters who could not ship direct to England traded their tobacco for articles from the stocks of clothing, tools, and other necessities sent out by the house in England. In this way such towns as Oxford, Alexandria, Chestertown, and Yorktown became centers of trade for a few years giving way in the late Eighteenth Century to Norfolk and Baltimore, the only ports today (except Newport News) of first rate importance.

Norfolk, created in 1680 as a paper town, had little reason for existence in the light of the times: its immediate hinterland was large but the soils were poor for tobacco, and for eight years its lots seemingly were not even laid out and it grew so slowly it had no need for a local government for over half a century. Norfolk did have a good harbor almost at the Bay entrance, close to parts of North Carolina where there were no deep-sea harbors at all, and when the planters in her own vicinity turned to products for which the land was suited she began to grow, an anomaly in the Bay Country, a trading town with a population composed of merchants (many of them Scots), mariners, and maritime craftsmen. Pine tar, pitch, turpentine, lumber of many kinds and forms, pork, and beef came from the Carolina Sounds. Tobacco in small driblets came too from

Carolina and from the smaller up river planters. Because many of these products were especially needed in the West Indies a large trade with the Islands sprang up, the lumber and foods exchanged for rum, molasses, sugar and slaves. The remainder of Norfolk's trade was largely with the Mother Country. In spite of the town's large English and Scotch population when the troubles with the British government began, most merchants took the American point of view. Consequently when late in August 1774 the brigantine *Mary and Jane* arrived with a consignment of tea, a meeting of the merchants unanimously resolved that the offensive article must be returned. Its consignees agreed without even a protest and Norfolk's tea party caused no troubles. When the War for Independence came, Norfolk was wide open for attack. On 1 January 1776 it came: H.M. ships *Liverpool, Otter,* and *Kingfisher* anchored off the town and began a bombardment followed by an assault. Both sides began to burn buildings and two days later the town was completely destroyed. At the end of the War the town was practically non-existent, its vessels were gone and its population scattered. Within a decade Norfolk was back on its feet, a crazy-quilt, jerry-built place to be sure, but booming, its trade with the French, Danish, and Dutch West Indies fully restored and despite British restrictions on trade with her islands, Jamaica, Antigua, and the Barbadoes, took every lading of lumber and food stuffs sent down. Wheat, too, was appearing in large quantities as the Virginia planters turned their worn out tobacco fields to grain. Since waterpower was not available Norfolk served as a collecting port and shipped the grain to the flouring mills elsewhere. Two of Virginia's own sons ended prosperity: President Jefferson with his embargo and President Madison with his war, neither of which suited Norfolk's traders. The city soon found itself under the guns of the British fleet again. This time she won. The peace treaty failed to provide a free West India trade and Norfolk sank to the status of a transshipment port where British ships brought in English goods, exchanged them for local products which were carried to the West Indies and traded for sugar, et cetera which went back to England. Only her coastal commerce was left, and the Civil War ended that. With the restoration of peace great changes took place in Norfolk's trade. Railways tapped a hinterland extending far into the South (which lacked good harbors) and into the mountains to the West. Cotton, almost unknown before the War, began to pour into Norfolk from the Carolinas and Georgia; coal came from

West Virginia. Both went to Europe as well as to the New England factory cities. Peanuts, vegetables, and small fruits came in by schooners and sloops for transshipment to markets in Boston, New York, Philadelphia, and Baltimore. Soon the port of Norfolk became too small to handle all its trade and spread to Newport News across Hampton Roads. Today the area under the control of a Port Authority is one of the world's great ports.

At the other end of the Bay from Norfolk, some fifty years later another paper town was created, Baltimore. Laid out by the surveyors in December 1730 it was the third town in Maryland to have the name and like its predecessors looked as if it might die at birth, for it was already surrounded by towns such as Elk Ridge Landing, Joppa, and others. Its hinterland was small, the harbor a miserable shallow stream, and tobacco continued to follow the old routes to the other towns. The first vessel in is said to have been able to load only one hogshead and in 1748 only eight vessels offered to haul freight out of the town. But Baltimore had one thing the others lacked, waterpower to drive the simple machinery that turned local grains into flour. One man, John Stevenson, lately an immigrant from Ireland, saw in flour a chance to help his none too well fed countrymen abroad; to encourage the tobacco planters to shift to grain on their worn out acres; and to turn a penny for himself. He loaded a vessel with Baltimore flour and sent her to Ireland. The venture proved successful in all three ways and when Stevenson died in 1785 the *Maryland Journal* said of him ". . . he was the first Exporter of Wheat and Flour from this port and consequently laid the foundation of its present commercial consequence." On that same flour and wheat Baltimore still depends for much of its life-blood.

Based on that trade, a small amount of tobacco, and on pig iron smelted from a local deposit of ore, Baltimore started to grow. In the 1750's German immigrants were taking up wheat lands north and west of the town; and others were opening shops and breweries in the town. At about the same time a large group of Acadians were literally tossed ashore near the shipyards at Fells Point. Many of them became shipcarpenters and mariners. One of the yards was that of George Wells, a builder of considerable ability, who during the War for Independence built the ship *Defence* for the Maryland State Navy and the frigate *Virginia* for the Continental Navy as well as several privateers and small men of war. Until David Stodder came to Baltimore after the war and built the 600 ton ship *Goliath* and the frigate *Constellation*, Wells was the leading shipwright.

By 1760 Baltimore had passed all of Maryland's one time chief ports, Annapolis, Oxford, and Chestertown, whose maritime tradesmen were removing to the busier town. Ten years later Baltimore had its own marine insurance underwriters, evidence of steady, sustained shipping activity. When the port of Boston was closed by the British, she was wealthy enough to send relief in the form of 3,000 bushels of corn, 20 barrels of rye, and 21 barrels of bread while Annapolis could only raise 1,000 bushels of corn and Chestertown but lend the vessel to transport the cargo. When war came, although Baltimore actually untouched by enemy action, her trade was closely blockaded and many of the shipping merchants directed their energies to manufacturing. Linen mills, nail mills, and ropewalks joined the flour and saw mills.

After Yorktown when the blockade of the Bay was lifted, Baltimore once more turning to the sea, quickly learned her harbor was far from adequate, and so shallow large vessels could come no closer than Fells Point, some little distance from the town itself. That meant expensive transshipment by lighters to reach the wharves. Under pressure from the merchants the mayor appointed a Board of Port Wardens who were given full authority over the harbor. Their first task was to survey and to chart. When they knew what was needed, they sent to Amsterdam for models and plans of a "mud machine" as the crude spoon dredges of the time were called. One was built locally and put to work deepening the channels and the Basin, the spoil being sold to fill in low ground for additional wharfage. To defray more of the costs a tonnage tax was levied on all vessels entering the harbor. After the adoption of the Federal Constitution that tax violated the interstate and foreign commerce clause, but Congress knowing it could not contribute itself and that the tax was in public interest, passed a legalizing act. With an adequate harbor trade boomed, particularly with the West Indies, flour, lumber, tobacco, and provisions going out and rum, molasses, raw sugar, and coffee back. Sugar refineries and distilleries were built to process the far larger quantities than Baltimore could use herself. Domestic exports totaled $3,600,000 in 1805; foreign products reexported totaled $10,900,000. Although Baltimore had an early introduction to the Oriental trade with John O'Donnell's ship *Pallas* in 1785, the continuation of the direct trade was comparatively small. She found buying

at Isle de France more profitable: there was a shorter tie-up of capital;
there were no troublesome Chinese trade customs to face; and the
sale of East India prizes at Isle de France provided India and China
goods cheaper than original cost. Besides at home the market
preferred West India coffee to Chinese tea. That preference was
made even stronger when in 1793 a fleet of 53 vessels arrived at
Baltimore bringing hundreds of French refugees from the great black
revolt in Hispaniola. Most of them settled in the town and became a
prominent part of the community taking up their old professions, the
Chatards their medicine; the Despeaux, Salenaves, de Rochebrunes,
and Descandes their shipbuilding.

Prosperity lasted until Jefferson's embargo, with flour the basis of
trade. When the War of 1812 began the old conservative merchants
wanted little of it, but the more venturesome quickly had privateers,
the fast "Baltimore Flyers," as the clippers were called at first, at sea.
A British blockade soon had the slower (not all the local vessels were
of clipper model) merchant fleet bottled up, and just as in 1776
many turned to manufacturing using waterpower, now flour mills,
saw and cotton mills were started this time driven by steam engines.

When peace came in 1815 Baltimore found the British ready to
dump goods, buy flour and tobacco, move on to the West Indies pick
up rum and sugar, and return home. She had to worry along with
only the local and coastal trade and had a very small bit of foreign
trade. Two years later European crops failed and a huge demand for
flour and provisions developed which got Baltimore off to a new
start on the high seas. Soon her ships were on the routes not only to
the West Indies and Europe but also to the East and West Coasts of
South America, bringing back copper ore and guano from around
the Horn; coffee and hides from Rio. By Mid-Century her merchant
marine was reaching a size undreamed of in 1800; the Baltimore and
Ohio Railroad, Baltimore's answer to the Erie Canal, was bringing
in grain and coal from the West; the Bay steamboats touching every
tributary brought vast supplies of food to the harbor; the Merchants
and Miners and other coastal lines organized in part by local capital
carried away the tanned hides, cottons, chemicals, and metals returning with shoes and other finished manufactures, which Baltimore
distributed South and West. Prosperity looked perpetual.

As suddenly as a blown fuse cuts off an electric light, Baltimore's
water born trade ended: the Civil War had begun and General Ben
Butler in command of Yankee troops held the city like a Genghis

Khan. Slowly permission was gained for some of the steamboats to resume limited operations in the Bay, but no foreign trade was allowed and the factories were turned to the production of military supplies, among them the plates for the building of the U.S.S. *Monitor*. When the war ended, Baltimore fortunately had no carpet-bag interlude and along the old familiar lines restarted its trade at once, even attempting to extend it with a Baltimore and Ohio line of steamers to Liverpool. That had no sound economic foundation and soon failed. But a contract with the North German Lloyd Line succeeded with flour and tobacco going out, toys and immigrants by the thousands coming in. That trade lasted until World War I. By that time Baltimore had twelve steamer lines serving fifteen ports in Britain and Europe. In 1920 there were forty lines entering Baltimore. Today with equipment second to none for handling coal, ores, fruit, grain and general merchandise; with eighty steamship services touching all the world's ports; with complete shipbuilding and repair facilities; Baltimore has become the nation's second port in volume of overseas trade handled, and leading the list of exports are John Stevenson's grain and flour.

The rise and decline of Oxford as a port is typical of the majority of those around the Bay. Little more than changes of dates and names would be necessary to make this the story of any of the small today but once important Bay Country towns.

In 1669 Lord Baltimore ordained "for the good of trade . . . certain ports . . . be appointed for the lading and unlading of merchandize . . ." Oxford was one of the ten ports thus established. If any settler moved into the town, no record of it has been preserved. Fourteen years later another act recreated the town and this time lots were taken up but by speculators and no town developed. In 1694 another act erected the town and required that the collector of customs live there. The next year, hoping for a change of luck, the town name became Williamstadt. Soon at least one merchant set himself up in business and the town was made a part of the intercolonial postal system. After the death of King William the name reverted to Oxford and in 1707 a wide customs district was set up with Oxford its collection point. Then the town began to grow: Gildart & Co., Foster, Cunliffe & Co., both of Liverpool, and Anthony Bacon of London established factories. A shipyard capable of building tobacco ships was in operation. The custom house books show direct trade with London, Liverpool, and Bristol; with Spain, Madeira,

Africa; and with Boston, New York, Philadelphia, Salem, Falmouth (Portland), and Nantucket. Early outbound cargoes include tobacco, furs, black walnut lumber and the inbound English manufactures, India goods, sugar, molasses, fruit, rum, wines, and slaves. Later exports added wheat, corn, pork, live stock and poultry, sassafras, shingles, staves, hoops, and bricks. Additions to the population came with almost every vessel and especially large ones in 1717 and 1745 when Scotch rebels were sent over and again in 1755 when many of the Acadians were brought in. Along with the factories of the English merchants, many local merchants had stores in the town and there were public warehouses for tobacco and salt. There was a direct packet line to the provincial capital, horse races, and seemingly theatrical performances. On the eve of the War for Independence Oxford was a port well in the fore of all those in the American Colonies.

Even so, the seeds of decline had already been sown. The leader of the town's commercial activities, Robert Morris, senior, father of the war-time financier, was killed in an accident, and was replaced by a man of far fewer attainments. Several of the foreign merchants withdrew from the declining tobacco trade and sold or closed their factories. Baltimore, full of energy, was rising at the expense of all the older ports taking the foreign trade and serving as a collection point for the commodities of the greater part of the Bay Country. The war with the virtual blockade by the British and Tory fleets, brought complete stagnation for almost a decade. As late as 1798 there were still a few foreign entries, but by 1800 there were less than one hundred persons, black and white, living in the town. Like his namesake of Biblical days, Captain Jeremiah Banning, of Oxford, who had skippered vessels to Madeira, London, the West Indies, Portugal, and Senegal, in 1793 lamented "Oxford whose streets and strands were once covered by busy noisy crowds ushering in commerce from almost every quarter of the globe is now shaded by wheat, corn and tobacco. The once well worn streets are now grown up in grass, save a few narrow tracks made by swine and sheep; and the strands have more the appearance of an uninhabited island than where human feet have ever trod."

The captain's song may be literally true for in 1825 it was actually necessary to resurvey the streets. For forty years the vegetation continued, and almost all that remained of Oxford's former glories was what Captain Banning called its "salubrious air".

Rebirth came at the end of the Civil War with the rise of the
Bay's oyster fishery. A packing house was opened; then a cannery.
Nathaniel Leonard started a shipyard, a saw and a grist mill. A
railroad was extended to the town. And in 1879 the first of a steadily
growing stream of Northerners bought a farm on the waterfront
where the salubrious air and unrivaled sailing could be enjoyed.
Today there are more vessels, yachts to be sure, anchored off the
Strand than ever Captain Banning saw. Perhaps they enter from
Long Island Sound or Marblehead instead of Funchal, Bristol, or
Goree. No cargoes of madeira wines, cotton goods, or blacks, are
under their hatches, but they have brought renewed life and prosperity
to the old port.

Jeremiah Banning's Custom House, Oxford District, 1789-1798. Photograph by
Mrs. John Woodall.

The Town and Port of Oxford, Maryland. At the bottom is drawn a trading sloop. Colored ink drawing on parchment by William Turbutt, 1707, owned by the Commissioners of Oxford.

Oxford, Maryland, today, orientation as in the 1707 plat. Photograph by H. Robins Hollyday.

Gloucester, Virginia, 1755. Note the similarity of the sloops to that in the Oxford Plat. Water colored drawing, owned by The Mariners' Museum.

Yorktown, Virginia, 1755. The lateen rigged boat is of especial interest. Water colored drawing, owned by The Mariners' Museum.

Alexandria, Virginia. Colored lithograph by Charles Magnus, New York, 1863. owned by The Mariners' Museum.

Annapolis, Maryland. Colored lithograph by Charles Magnus, New York, 1864, owned by The Mariners' Museum.

Baltimore. Lithograph by Edward Weber & Co., Baltimore, ca. 1840, owned by The Maryland Historical Society.

Baltimore, view of Federal Hill, Fardy & Auld shipyard, the signal station atop the hill and shipping are shown. Daguerreotype, ca. 1853, owned by The Peale Museum.

Model of a Spoon Dredge of the type used to deepen Baltimore Harbor. Power was supplied by the two tread mills. Model in the Musée de Marine, Paris.

Baltimore, the Basin, about 1865. Many of the late Eighteenth Century warehouses are still standing, and the shipping includes pungies, a scow sloop, several schooners and Bay steamboats. Photograph owned by The Peale Museum.

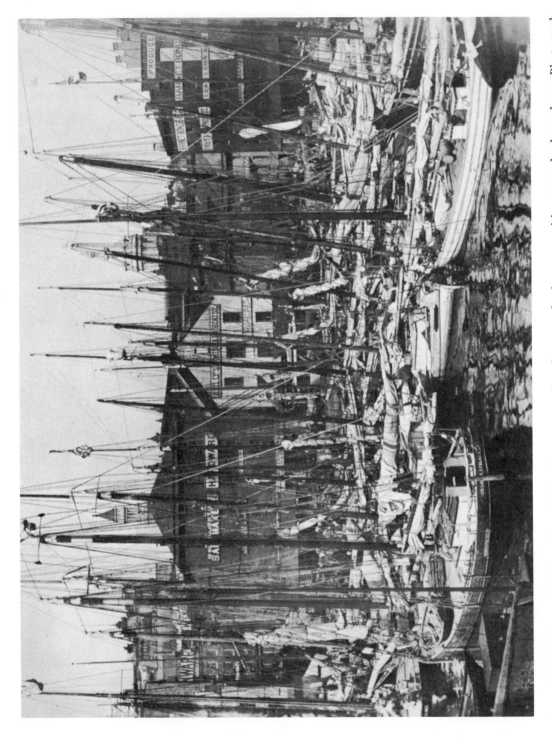

Baycraft in Baltimore Harbor, about 1890. Bugeyes, pungies, sloops, and schooners waiting to unload produce. Photograph owned by The United States National Museum.

Norfolk and Portsmouth, Virginia, with views of Old Point Comfort and the Navy Yard. Lithograph by E. Sachse, Baltimore, 1851, owned by The Mariners' Museum.

The International Naval Rendezvous at Hampton Roads, Virginia, 1893. Colored lithograph, owned by The Mariners' Museum.

Fortress Monroe and the Hygeia Hotel, Old Point Comfort, Virginia. Right foreground is the Old Bay Line steamboat *Adelaide*. Colored lithograph by E. Sachse & Co., 1861, owned by The Mariners' Museum.

Georgetown, Maryland, ca. 1906. Two grain schooners, a freight steamer, and the passenger steamboat *Van Corlear the Trumpeter,* at the wharves. Photograph owned by The United States National Museum.

Cambridge, Maryland, with oyster fleet at the wharves.
Photograph by M. V. Brewington, 1948.

Crisfield Harbor, dredge boats waiting to get up to packing houses.
Photograph by Frank A. Moorshead, 1918.

Tangier Island, Virginia. Photograph by A. C. Brown, about 1938.

Newport News, Virginia. Schooners and barges at the coal docks, 1900. Photograph owned by The Mariners' Museum.

Opening of the dry dock at Gosport (Norfolk) Navy Yard, 1833. Lithograph after Joseph Goldsborough Bruff. owned by The Mariners' Museum.

The U.S.S. *Delaware*, the first vessel to enter the dry dock at Norfolk Navy Yard. Lithograph after J. G. Bruff, 1833, owned by The Mariners' Museum.

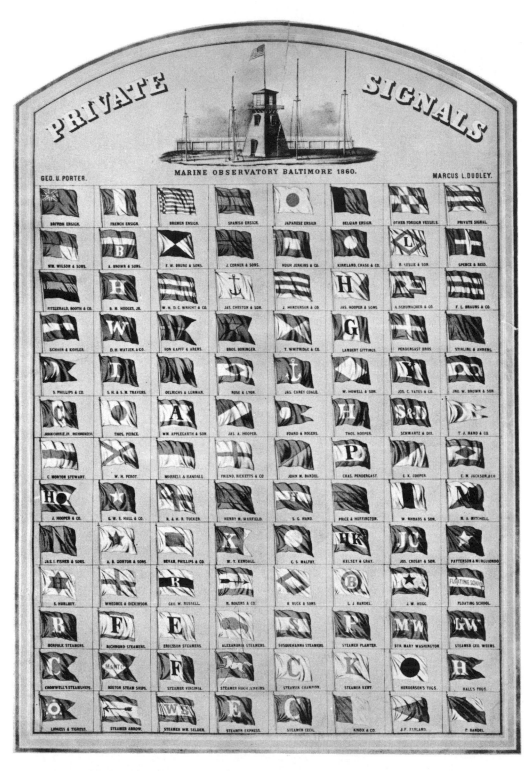

Signals of the Chesapeake Bay shipping merchants, with a view of the signal station on Federal Hill, Baltimore. Colored lithograph, 1860, owned by The Maryland Historical Society.

VIII.

Commerce and Trade

ONCE the gold and pearl seeking fever satiated itself by none being found, the Virginia colonists began to send home a few furs, cedar and walnut board, sassafras root (a sure cure for the King's disease), "pych", pickled sturgeon and "cavyarge", as one colonist spelled caviar, and in return received almost everything needed for pioneer living. In 1614 Virginia tobacco cultivated by John Rolfe perhaps with the aid of his wife Pocahantas was found to be as good as that from Trinidad and within five years dominated the trade of the Bay. By 1697, 36,750,000 pounds were being exported to England, requiring 150 ships to carry it. How much more was smuggled out to evade the export duties and the number of illicit trading vessels carrying it is of course unrecorded but the numbers must have been large, for in 1637 the first custom house was set up in Virginia to watch the quantity shipped so that it might be checked against the quantity received in the British Isles. Until the Civil War tobacco ruled the life of the lower Bay Country, particularly Virginia, serving not only as the principal commodity but also as the local currency.

Maryland early in the Eighteenth Century found that in some of its counties wheat could be grown equally as profitably as tobacco and that its production did not ruin the soil as tobacco did. Furthermore, the flour made from Maryland wheat, it was discovered, did not mildew in the tropics as rapidly as wheat grown in the Northern colonies. Thenceforth much of the foreign as well as Bay trade was based on flour and grain. These served as the export base for the South American coffee and copper ore trades which Baltimore controlled during the Nineteenth Century.

The mills which furnished flour for export were not all large city factories driven by steam or water power. The number of wind powered mills around the Bay is unknown but must have been large: there were nineteen along the Great and Little Choptank Rivers and there were 392 flour and grist mills of all types in Maryland in 1850. Another type of mill, less frequently found than wind mills, depended for its power on the ebb and flow of the tide through a narrow sluice into a large landlocked bay. While the grinding capacity of any one wind or tide mill was small, their combined production was an important factor in the Bay's supply of flour for export.

The rapid soil exhaustion caused by the continuous growing of tobacco and cotton was responsible for another trade in which the Bay ports led for many years. To restore the fertility fish and animal manures were first used on the fields but the quantities of these available were insufficient. Early in the Ninetenth Century the value of the vast guano deposits in some of the West India Islands and in South America was realized and in 1832 a small quantity was brought to the Bay Country from Peru. It proved to be highly successful. Twenty years later Baltimore was supplying the entire Southern United States with fertilizer largely composed of guano. New deposits were being sought constantly and in 1856 Congress passed an act enabling our citizens to take possession of any unclaimed island or key where deposits were found and the importation of guano was considered as part of the coastal trade. Navassa Island, a small key between Cuba and Jamaica, became almost a suburb of Baltimore, and it is said police magistrates offered prisoners a choice of working in Navassa or serving time in the local jail.

The slave trade began in 1619, almost simultaneously with that in tobacco. A Dutch privateer, sailing under a commission from the Prince of Orange, is said to have brought in the first lading. Along with her and carrying some negroes also came the *Treasurer,* owned in part at least by Sir Samuel Argoll, recently governor of Virginia. It is believed with some justification that these first negroes were sold as servants, not as slaves. Up to 1662 the Dutch were the chief importers and enjoyed special export duty exemptions on tobacco when slaves were imported. After that date the Royal African Company was given the sole right to import slaves which were ordered from England in the same manner as merchandise. Some smuggling by "interlopers," that is, by others than the Company, also went on. For instance, the ship *Society* of Bristol claiming she was short of provisions came in on the Eastern Shore and landed 120 negroes which were sold for the non-payment of duties. Others were brought in from the West Indies and the Carolinas where the trade exceeded that with the Bay Colonies many fold. But locally-born negroes always were considered better than imports because they were acclimated and less subject to epidemic diseases. Since slaves were valuable property, they were almost uniformly well cared for, and their natural increase, plus a few imports provided for most of the needs. Long after the American slave trade had been ended, one contact continued with the Bay: her fast clipper vessels were much in demand by Spanish and Portuguese slavers because they were the only vessels which had a chance of evading the British and American patrols on the African and South American coasts. After 1834 Maryland serving as the base of operations of the American Colonization Society which had purchased and organized a part of the West Coast of Africa as the "State of Maryland in Liberia", sent back hundreds of manumitted slaves and free negroes. Eight specially built vessels (1 ship, 2 barks, 1 brig, and 4 schooners) owned, and many others chartered, by the Society ran from Baltimore as packets to Monrovia loaded with passengers, tools, and other supplies. There was little similarity between the slavers and the Liberian packets. The *Mary Caroline Stevens* built in Baltimore by Abrahams & Ashcroft in 1856 had a cabin for sixteen passengers "furnished in a style which will compare with the finest European passenger ships." Her 'tween decks exclusively for emigrants was arranged "in the very best and most desirable manner, in accordance with the requirements of the late United States passenger law, and will render them as comfortable as any steerage passengers can be."

Add pig iron to tobacco, wheat, and lumber and the important early exports are covered. There were others, of course, for instance King William ordered "100 Mocking Birds, Blew Birds, Baltimore Birds, Black Birds and Red Wings" sent over, but such articles made little or no change in the export figures. It is interesting to note that in 1621 Virginia had an arrival from the East Indies, the ship *Royal James*, but from then on until John O'Donnell came into Baltimore with the ship *Pallas* in 1785, no other Oriental trade is known. In-bound cargoes were largely made up of manufactured goods which the colonies were unable to produce themselves thanks to the mercantile policy of the Mother Country. Wine from the Madeiras and Spain, fruit, rum, and sugar from the West Indies were allowed to enter. Later coffee, hides, and copper ore were added to the list. These same products with a steady lessening of the proportion of manufactured goods as we began to make our own, have remained the chief articles of trade. Grains and flour, metals and tobacco still lead the exports: Scotch whiskey has taken the place of wines and products unknown to our ancestors, chrome, manganese, petroleum, have appeared on the import list. But substantially the character of the foreign trade of the Bay is unchanged.

The early coastal trade followed much the same pattern as the foreign trade. Virginia had its beginning with tobacco and Maryland its start by sending Indian corn to New England in trade for salt fish. Both were soon trading with the Dutch at New Amsterdam, and the Swedes on the Delaware as well, with European goods the import. No great change in the character of the Bay's coastal trade came until the late 1870's and early 1880's. By then the industrialization of the North Atlantic States was well under way and vast quantities of coal were needed for steam and gas production. The Baltimore and Ohio, the Western Maryland, and Northern Central Railways had all been extended from Baltimore to the coal mines of Maryland, Pennsylvania, and West Virginia; the Chesapeake and Ohio came into Newport News and the Norfolk and Western into Norfolk. All of them built more or less automatic coal loading piers at their tidewater termini. Hundreds of vessels, at first small schooners, then as trade expanded three masters, four, five, six and even one seven master, were coming to the Bay ports for coal to be carried chiefly to the New England factory cities. In the early days cargoes of ice came down to the Bay from the ponds of Maine and Massachusetts. Even small river ports such as Salisbury received almost their only supplies from the coal schooners which when unloaded sailed light to the coal piers at Baltimore or Hampton Roads. As artificial ice plants were established the trade ended and the colliers moved South light. In 1899 Newport News loaded 1904 schooners with Baltimore and Norfolk together approximately as many more. Tow boats and barges replaced schooners and steamers the barges but the trade still continues.

Within the Bay, towns no longer self-sufficient began to develop a trade pattern: grain, lumber, cordwood, oysters, and farm products went by small schooners and sloops to Norfolk and Baltimore, Richmond and Annapolis. They sent back manufactured goods, fertilizer, and political gossip. Up to the end of World War I it was not uncommon for the proprietors of general stores in the Bay or river towns to own one or more vessels which carried local produce to the city markets, returning with molasses, kerosene, sugar, clothing, hardware, and frequently passengers. In fact there were many families who owning a vessel made semi-annual trips to the City to do all their buying, go to the theater, and visit relatives, never going to their county seat except to serve on the jury, or to sue a neighbor.

The full extent of the Bay trade can never be calculated because no custom house entries were required. Some indication can be gained from the counts of arrivals at Baltimore made by Judge Thomas Jones who lived near the harbor entrance. In 1789 he saw 67 ships, 176 brigs, 396 sea sloops and schooners and 3,941 Baycraft enter the port. In 1812 he counted 181 ships, 168 brigs, 508 sea sloops and schooners, and 7,268 Baycraft. The Baycraft averaged 191 each day. What may have been happening in the other ports is not known. The coming of the steamboat to the Bay made no change in the character of the trade, it was simply speeded, and products such as soft crabs, fresh fish, and strawberries, which because of the uncertainty of sailing craft could not be sent to the cities from distant points began to move in volume. Once motor vehicles became commonplace, the Bay trade virtually ended. Today a few motor vessels in place of hundreds of sailing craft haul grain, fertilizer, slag for road building and oil products, more value and tonnage perhaps than the Bay ever saw before but the stench and sound of a diesel exhaust can hardly compare with the anchors coming to the cat heads and the halliard blocks cackling as the crews sang:

O a hundred years ain't a very long time
On the Eastern Sho'
O way-O
Look out gal, I'm comin' home
To the Eastern Sho'
O way-O

Seal of the Collector of Customs, Oxford ca. 1785-89. Owned by
The Maryland Historical Society.

Transporting tobacco from plantation to ship. A. double canoe, B. lighter,
C. wagon, D. rolling. From Tatham: *Historical and Practical Essay on . . . Tobacco.*
London, 1800. Owned by Colonial Williamsburg Inc.

Planter selling tobacco. From Fry and Jefferson: *Map of Virginia,* 1775, owned by The Peabody Museum, Salem.

Tobacco being landed in England in the Eighteenth Century. Engraving at The Mariners' Museum.

Eighteenth Century English and Dutch tobacco package labels. Engravings at The Mariners'
Museum, and the last owned by M. V. Brewington.

The Curing and Storage of Tobacco. a, The common Tobacco House. b, Tobacco hanging upon a scaffold. c, The operation of prizing. d, Inside view of a Tobacco House, shewing the tobacco hanging to cure. e, An outside view of public warehouses. f, An inside view of the public warehouse, shewing the process of inspection. From Tatham: *Historical and Practical Essay on . . . Tobacco.* London, 1800. Owned by Colonial Williamsburg, Inc.

Wheat being loaded on a bugeye in Swan Creek, Harford County, Maryland about 1906. Photograph by H. Osborne Michael.

Wheat loading from farm wagon to skiff, Tred Avon River, Maryland, 1915.

Wheat being transferred from skiff to schooner. Photographs by H. Robins Hollyday.

Grain elevator at Locust Point, Baltimore, 1872 with Baycraft waiting to unload. Photograph in The Maryland Historical Society.

Tide mill on Mobjack Bay, Virginia. Photograph by Raymond
Spears, 1904.

Post type windmill at Woolford,
Maryland about 1900. Photograph
owned by M. V. Brewington.

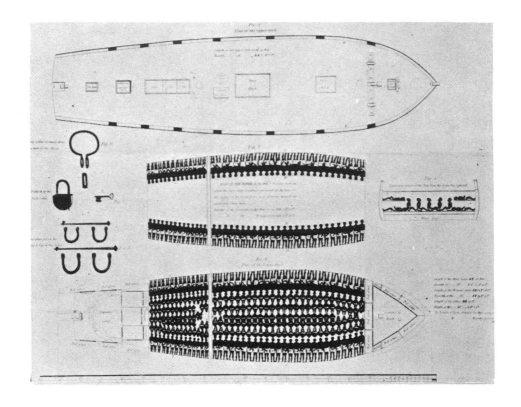

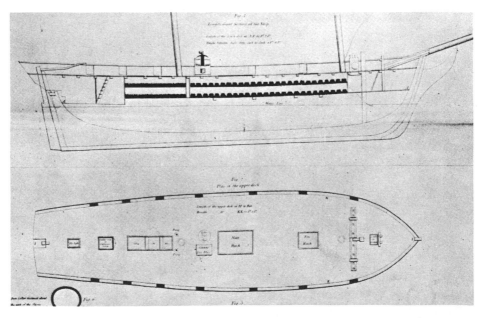

Method of stowing slaves on a Clipper brig, 1822. Engraved plans owned by The
Peabody Museum, Salem.

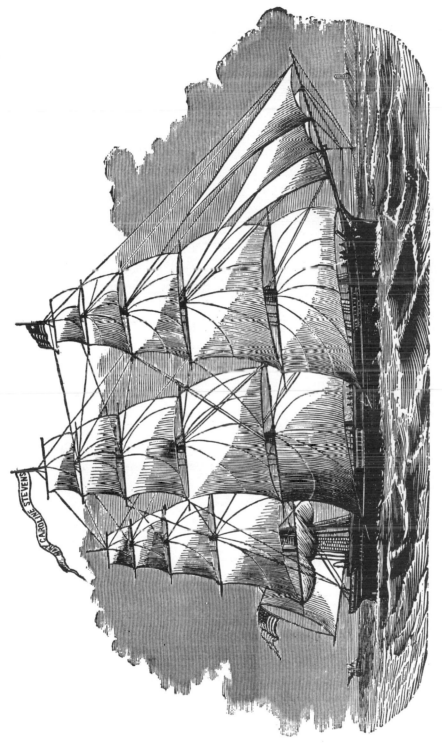

Ship *Mary Caroline Stevens*, built by Abrahams & Ashcraft, at Baltimore, 1856, to carry negroes to Liberia. Woodcut owned by The Maryland Historical Society.

Ram *Levin J. Marvel,* built at Bethel, Delaware, 1891, loaded with lumber. Photograph by Frank
A. Moorshead, Jr., 1938.

Ram *Edwin R. Baird, Jr.,* built at Bethel, Delaware, 1903, unloading lumber in Baltimore.
Photograph by Frank A. Moorshead, Jr., 1938.

Schooner *Mildred* loaded with lumber. Photograph by Frank A. Moorshead, Jr.

Bay schooner loaded with lumber. Photograph owned by The Peale Museum.

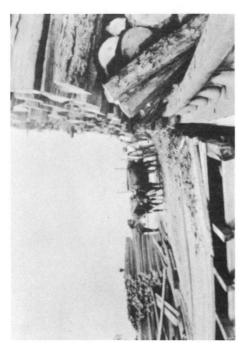

Loading cordwood on schooner *Gracie May*, Piankatank River, Virginia, 1911. Photographs by H. Osborne Michael.

Strawberries waiting for the steamboat, Nanticoke, Maryland, 1915 Photograph by William Willing.

Cord wood pier in Baltimore ca. 1900. Photograph owned by H. Osborne Michael.

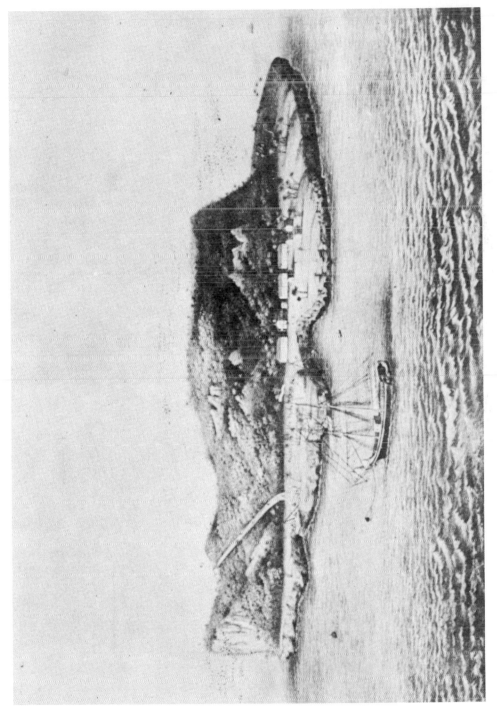

The Baltimore suburb Navassa Island, ca. 1880. Note the great flocks of sea-birds flying over the Island, the worker's barracks, and the open anchorage for the guano vessels. Photograph owned by The Maryland Historical Society.

Ore ship unloading at Curtis Bay ore pier, Baltimore, 1950.

IX.

Maritime Artisans

SHIPCARPENTERS are by no means the only workmen involved in getting a new vessel to sea or keeping her in service. There are caulkers who with specialized tools make a hull water tight. Around the Bay the trade, to a large extent, but not wholly, was in the hands of negroes either as slaves or freemen. One of the greatest of that race, Frederick Douglass, was once a caulker in Maryland shipyards before his rise to fame. It is a trade which has seen very few changes in either work methods or in gear and it is likely those who came over in 1610 would be equally competent workmen today without a refresher course.

There were sailmakers, but seemingly that trade did not appear around the Bay for many years after shipbuilding was well established. There were none in the group of maritime artisans who came over with Sir Thomas Gates. In the earliest period sails already made up were imported from England or the Netherlands for the majority of the larger vessels and for many of the smaller ones. Who may have made the sails for the others is not recorded, for some sails were made since the Maryland colonists were instructed to bring with them cloth for sails and even before that Claiborne bought "canvis" for the sails of his Bay-built trading vessels. The first recorded sailmaker was an Irish indentured servant who in 1736 ran away from his master if not from his job. There were four in Norfolk in 1776 and 119 in Baltimore in 1850. Today less than half a dozen are known to be following their trade in the whole Bay Country.

There were carvers. They also came late—in 1757 figureheads were still being imported, chiefly from New England, and fifteen years later vessels built on speculation for sale in England carried no decorations so that the new owner might add them to suit his taste. When the frigate *Constellation* was built in Baltimore in the late 1790's the carved work was executed in Philadelphia by William Rush, who sent one of his workmen, John Brown, to fit the pieces to the vessel. He remained in Baltimore for some years and seems to have become the leading shipcarver. Actually as long as the Baltimore Clipper type dominated there was little chance for the use of carved work for excess weight was not wanted, consequently all of it was small and light. This trend continued and in the last days of shipcarving, say after 1865, Baycraft have adopted a design more or less their own. Heads are small, comparatively speaking, and subordinate to the trail-boards; both are designed to be seen broadside. Stern decorations also are small and light, a star, a fraternal emblem, a spread eagle, or perhaps a bust, and as often as not these are painted rather than carved. One type of piece appears to have been unique in America: the mast head figure. These were full round but diminutive figures, a winged horse, a person, a foul anchor, placed atop the bald foremasts of schooners and pungies. Although local carvers appeared later than in other areas, they have lasted longer—there are still several semi-professionals who design and execute trailboards, figureheads, or other decorations.

Ropemakers as professionals had appeared in 1610, but little or nothing is heard of them for over a century. Attempts to grow hemp were made in both Bay colonies without commercial success and although several ropewalks were established in Maryland in the 1740's and slightly later in Virginia, leading vessel owners continued to import their cordage from England until the War for Independence, complaining that the local product was of poor quality. During the War it came from France and Holland via the West Indies. After the War, ropemaking flourished on supplies of hemp from the Baltic. The Map of Baltimore published in 1792 shows the walks scattered all about the city wherever a space long enough could be found, and in 1850, 119 ropemakers were at work.

Coopers were important men around the Bay from the Mid-Seventeenth Century not primarily for water, beer and rum containers, but for tobacco hogsheads. Every plantation of any size had its own cooper-age shop, and after grain milling began, barrel factories were started. Since the man who made a tobacco cask or flour barrel could with a little extra care turn out a water butt, there was no difficulty furnishing vessels and few records have been kept. It as a trade, although fully mechanized, still continues to turn out flour, fish, and crab barrels, and tobacco hogsheads.

The shipsmith's is another trade which has also lived in the Bay Country. The rise of the auto might have spelled doom for the man who only shod horses, mules and oxen and repaired wagons, but not for the shipsmith. They may not have many gammon irons to make today or many deadeyes to strop, but the smiths have grapnels and net anchors to make; tong and nipper heads; and dredges to build and repair. There are many fewer smiths at work today, but those who are have more than enough business to keep them going. One smith has attained nation-wide reputation and builds dredges of many designs for use wherever oysters are caught with that device. Another shipsmith's business has developed into a nationally known firm making tongs, nippers, crab net bows, the dozen or so types of oyster and crab knives, and fine table cutlery.

Several trades whose products were closely allied with shipbuilding have disappeared and because they were usually followed by country people as spare time work, little record of any sort has survived. One was the trunnel, or tree-nail makers, who with a froe, mallet, and blocks of locust, split out, and shaved into "eight-square" (octagonal) shape the wooden pegs with which a vessel's planking was held to her frame in the days before iron spikes were plentiful. In the Seventeenth and Eighteenth Centuries the business was large enough to show considerable exports to Great Britain, one plantation sent 70,000 trunnels at one time. Two types of machine were eventually devised to make trunnels and with them the hand industry disappeared. Another industry was that of the mast hoop and jib hank maker, who with draw knife, axe, and shaving bench split out hickory, oak, and ash rods, which, bent into hoops of various sizes, held the fore and aft sails to masts or stays. With the decline in the number of sailing vessels his trade too has disappeared. Two other home industries were making trunnel wedges and sheathing nail plugs. The wedges were driven into the outer end of each trunnel to expand it and so increase its holding power. Making them disappeared with the trunnel. Sheathing nail plugs are still in use on the remaining Bay vessels which, although their bottoms are coated with copper paint instead of copper plates, continue to cover the waterline area with sheet metal as an ice protection. When a vessel has her metal replaced each nail hole from the old covering is plugged with a wooden pin. Splitting out these little matchstick sized plugs was once a fairly common home industry, and some are still made, but if around the Bay the makers are too well hidden for a camera to find.

Once the shipbuilders and the other artisans turned a new vessel over to the owners, seamen and navigators were needed. If the number of schools which offered to teach navigation is a criterion, then most of the Eighteenth Century males around the Bay knew something of it. A few evidently knew a great deal about the art for when the British Parliament offered a huge prize to anyone who could "discover the longitude," one Eastern Shoreman announced that he had succeeded where Europe's greatest mathematicians and astronomers had failed, but never did he give it to the eagerly waiting world, nor did he attempt to claim the prize. Another Bayman preceded Nathaniel Bowditch in compiling an *American Practical Navigator* by many years but his work failed to find a publisher.

During most of the Seventeenth Century navigators must have learned their art on board ship since schools did not exist until William and Mary College in Virginia and King William's School, now St. John's College, Annapolis, were founded in the 1690's. In the Eighteenth Century schools blossomed in Queen Anne County, at Upper Marlboro, London Town on South River, near Princess Anne, and Easton, Maryland and in several sections of Virginia, all of them teaching navigation. In the 1850's Baltimore organized a "Floating School" on board the retired sloop of war *Ontario* in which orphans were taught seamanship and navigation. To it the great oceanographer, Virginia-born Matthew F. Maury, presented 120 charts and a complete set of his works on navigation and oceanography. Seemingly it was the first school of its kind in America, the predecessor of today's maritime academies.

Near the *Ontario* another old hulk, that of the ship *Wm Penn,* served as a church or Bethel for the port's seafaring population. As early as the 1830's such a Bethel had existed and from then until the present, Baltimore has had a church specifically dedicated for the use of seamen and the maritime artisans. From the beginning the trustees have been the leading shipping merchants of the port. On the opposite side of the harbor another old hulk called the *Elephant* served jointly Baachus, Aphrodite, and Mammon with its patrons drawn from the newly paid-off seamen. In spite of steady police interest in the activities aboard the *Elephant* no picture of her is known to exist.

Albert E. Brown, sailmaker, Wenona, Maryland. Photograph by William T. Radcliffe.

David Pritchard, sailmaker, Oxford, Maryland. Photograph by Donald Ross.

Brown's sail loft, Wenona, Maryland. Photograph by M. V. Brewington.

Sailmaker's tools, owned
by M. V. Brewington.

A. Seaming palm.
B. Roping palm.
D. Seam rubber.
E. Knives.
F. Knife sharpening stone.
G. Needle sharpening stone.
H. Packing needle.
I. Short-square needle.
J. Long-square needle.
K. Needle packages.
L. Needle horn.
M. & N. Needle cases.
O. Bees wax.
P. Sail twine.
Q. Bench hooks.
R. Chalk line and reel.
S. Drawing dividers.
T. Heavers.
U. Grommet setters.
V. Pricker.
W. Marline spike.
X. Splicing fid.
Z. Measurement book.

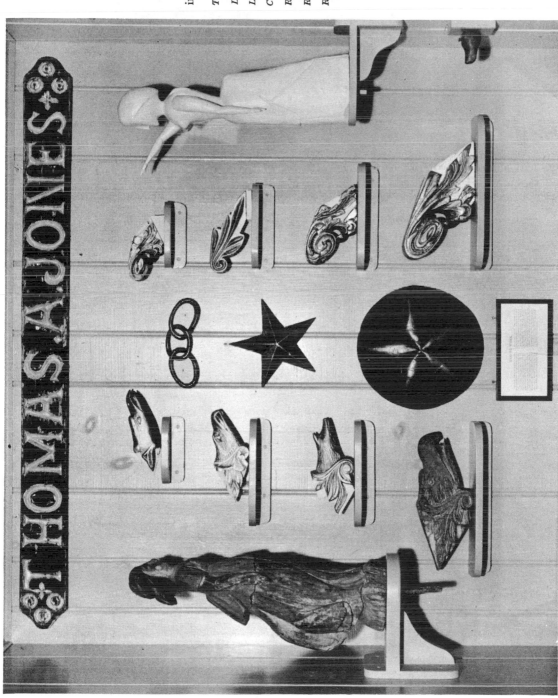

Chesapeake Bay ship carvings, owned by M. V. Brewington.

Top: Name board schooner *Thomas A. Jones,* 1911.

Left: Mast head figure Pungy *Mary J. Bond,* 1874.

Left center: Figure heads, 1853-1900.

Center: Stern decorations, 1885-1920.

Right center: Billet heads, 1856-1915.

Right: Figure head found afloat in Fishing Bay about 1890.

Right bottom: Figure head canoe *Bull Dog,* 1880.

[163]

Stern carving, pungy *Amanda F. Lewis,* 1884, probably carved by Hammond Skinner, owned by The United States National Museum.

Typical Chesapeake Bay trail board. Photograph by M. V. Brewington.

Caulker's and rigger's tools, owned by M. V. Brewington. Left to right: bottom scraper, bone fid and marline spike, three making irons, bottom scraper, bent garboard iron, deck iron, bottom scraper, reefing iron, rigger's belt with grease horn, marline spike and knife, caulker's mallet, serving board, boat caulking wheel, caulker's leather finger guard, serving board, hawsing iron.

Caulking a side seam.

Caulking a deck seam. Photographs by M. V. Brewington.

Chesapeake Bay shipcarpenter's tools, owned by M. V. Brewington. Joiner's plane, rabbet plane, auger, hawse hole compass, sparmaker's draw knife, spar 8-square guage, bevel square, Indian canoe-builder's tools, felling axe.

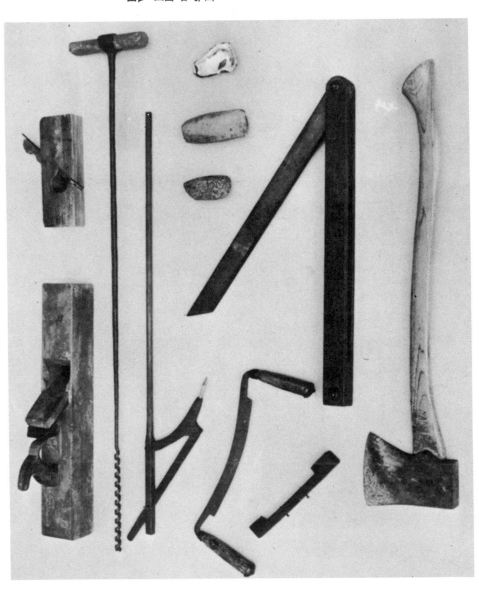

Shipcarpenter's tools. Brace and auger, right-hand broad axe, scorp for hollowing logs, smoothing p l a n e , beading plane, bol: set, race knife for marking timber, lip adze, hollow adze, plane adze, hollow slick, flat slick.

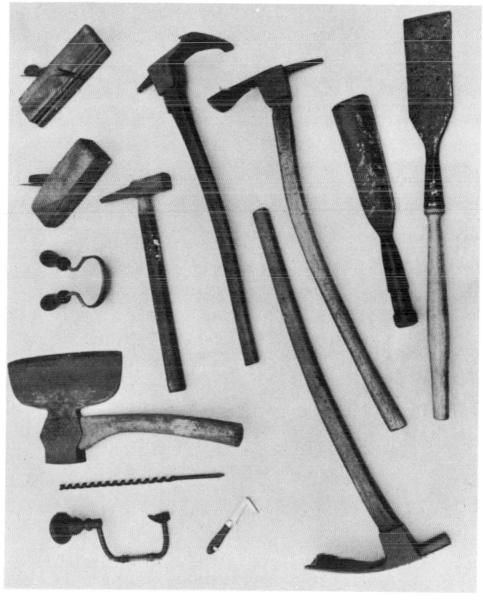

Trade card of a Baltimore nautical instrument dealer, ca. 1800, owned by The
United States Coast and Geodetic Survey.

Baltimore shipchandler's store, ca. 1890. Photograph owned by C. Harvey Merryman.

The *Ontario*, the floating school at Baltimore 1857. Woodcut owned by The Peale Museum.

The hulk of the ship *Wm Penn,* the Seamen's Bethel in Baltimore, 1846.

The interior of the Bethel during a service. Photographs owned
by The Maryland Historical Society.

X.

Oysters, Crabs, and Fish

ON THE second day in the New World, the exploring party ". . . came to a place where they [the Indians] had made a great fire and had beene newly a rosting Oysters . . . We eat some of the Oysters, which were very large and delicate in taste," wrote George Percy in 1607. From that day oysters have been a common but never tiring part of the Bay Country food. By 1737 catching oysters was a regular occupation. The first method of taking them was simply making a heap with a rake formed from a forked stick—the Indians were doing that when the settlers arrived. About the Mid-Seventeenth Century tongs came into use. These are a pair of long tined iron rakes with handles twelve to twenty feet long joined together like scissors. Just above the rake bars are baskets formed of iron rods. In use, the heads are lowered to the bottom, the handles opened and closed until a number of oysters are felt between the heads. Then the tongs are closed, thereby collecting the oysters in the baskets, raised into the boat, and the oysters dumped. In waters too deep for wooden shafts "patent" tongs made to work with ropes have been invented. In the 1880's over 6,000 tongers were working in the Bay and that tool still produces the majority of the catch. Small tongs—called "nippers" or "paws"—with shafts up to 10 feet long and heads about four inches wide are used in clear shallow waters for picking up single very large oysters called "coves" which bring a premium over bed oysters. The last tool, the one responsible for the development of the bugeye, is the dredge, or "drudge" as it is aptly named by the watermen. Brought to the Bay by New Englanders about 1800, the dredge was soon outlawed as it was believed to be destructive to the beds, but finally was legalized in 1865. At first it consisted of a wooden bar (later steel) with iron teeth along one side. To the bar was attached a bag made of rope netting held open by an iron frame, a bridle and a tow line. The dredge when in use was thrown over the side of the vessel and dragged along the bottom. The teeth

171

picked up oysters which collected in the bag. When the bag was filled, the dredge was hauled on deck by hand-turned winches called "winders" and the catch dumped. From one to four dredges were used, depending upon the size of the vessel. During the hey-day of the oyster fishery in the 1880's when over 18,000,000 bushels were caught, there were 2567 drudge boats (any vessel using a dredge is a "drudge boat") licensed on the Bay. Today there are less than 100, all still working under sail since power propelled craft are illegal as dredge boats in Maryland waters.

In the days of hand winders, dredging was hard and dangerous work; food and living conditions were poor; and since large crews were needed, it was difficult to man the vessels. Crimps soon became the chief suppliers of hands and as usual their methods of recruiting were none too scrupulous. Baltimore, Philadelphia, and New York were full of immigrants, most of them ignorant of our ways and language, all looking for work. Promises of easy jobs, good food, and high pay brought dozens to the Bay. Once aboard the dredge boats, the men were hazed without mercy. The word quickly spread and crimps' promises brought no hands. Then shanghai methods, free drinks till drunk, knockout drops, and the blackjack, were used to get a crew, and no man was safe around the Baltimore waterfront after dark in the R-months. Afloat the "paddies" as all immigrants were called, were beaten with belaying pins, brass knuckles, and slung shot to keep them at work and murder was not infrequent. If a paddy stayed (willingly or unwillingly) with a dredger long enough to have wages due him after all the deducts for grub, clothing, boots, tobacco and cakes at exhorbitant prices, he quite likely would be "paid off with the boom." That is, he would be ordered to some job on the cabin trunk, and the skipper would jibe the boom, knocking the paddy overboard, sometimes with a broken back. At last the German Society took up the fight against the crimps and dredge boat skippers. Its lawyers prosecuted many and finally managed to get an act of the Maryland legislature to protect the crews. But the political power of the watermen was so great the law was repealed and had to be replaced by Federal legislation.

Legalizing the dredge brought problems to Maryland: two groups of watermen with conflicting interests were created first of all; second, easily evadable restrictions were fixed and if the dignity of the law was to be upheld, there must be real enforcement. The two groups were tongers and dredgers. Neither of them could work on the others "rocks" (the natural oyster bed), the tongers, because the dredger's rocks were in too deep water; the dredgers, because the law said to them keep off the tonger's rocks. To enforce the law, in 1868 an "Oyster Navy" was established first with sloops and schooners armed with rifles, later with steamers carrying Dahlgren howitzers and Maxim rapid fire rifles. There were troubles every year but nothing serious was experienced until the 1880's. Then the price of oysters was high and the dredge fleet was skippered by men born without fear of man, God, or Devil. The trouble broke out when a fleet of dredge boats invaded Swan Point Bar off Rock Hall driving the tongers away by running their canoes down and shooting at them. Together with the townspeople the tongers mounted an old cannon on the point to cover their work. At night the dredgers landed and carried off the cannon. Next day there were 400 dredge boats on the bar. The sloop *Mary Compton* of the Oyster Navy appeared and as she approached, the near dredgers opened fire with rifles while the others continued working. The *Compton* answered with her cannon, but it took so long to reload the old muzzle loader, the dredgers with their Winchesters soon drove her off, and the *Compton* ran down the Bay with signals for help flying. These were answered by the police steamer *McLane*, though by the time she reached Swan Point the dredgers were gone. Since the sailing police boats were scarcely more heavily armed than the pirates little attention was paid to them until one of the steamers was sighted by the fast pungies deployed as lookouts by the dredgers. Battle after battle took place, with the dredgers always able to choose the spot. After the pirates had shot up a Baltimore steamboat which it is said was bringing a posse down the Bay to take the dredge boat skippers, Captain Thomas Contee Bowie Howard was put in command of the *McLane* with orders to stop the trouble. He caught the dredge fleet working a tongers' bar in the Chester River. With a voice that could be heard on the Western Shore, Captain Tom called on the fleet to surrender. The answer was a hail of bullets. Captain Tom rang up full speed ahead and rammed the nearest dredge boat. Backing off he rammed a second, then headed for a third. Every near dredger surrendered and the rest fled. Never again was there any serious trouble, but the Oyster Navy with the S.S. *Potomac* as flag ship still patrols the Bay and its rivers as soon as R appears in the calendar.

In the summer months when the Bay's waters begin to warm, oysters, although edible, begin to spawn, lose their flavor, and without refrigeration spoil quickly. But at the same time crabs emerge from their hibernation and move into shoal waters to feed and shed, and thence to the table replacing the soft and almost tasteless oyster. The early settlers found crabs a foot long and four inches wide commonplace; today such giants for some as yet unknown reason are caught only in the Miles and Wye Rivers with the ordinary crabs about half that size. Two methods are used commercially for taking crabs: the trot line in the rivers and the pot, or trap, in the Bay proper. The amateur crabber uses a hand line and a dipnet. A trot line is a heavy cotton cord up to a quarter mile long with a light anchor (a ten pound stone will do) and a gallon can for buoy at each end. Knotted to the line every five or six feet is a piece of bait—salted eel preferably or salted tripe second choice. When set, the line sinks to the bottom with the buoys showing its location. To the starboard side of the boat is attached an outrigger perhaps two feet long with a spool-shaped roller on its end. In the days of sail the line was put out directly across the path of the wind, so the skiff could reach from buoy to buoy and back without tacking. When all was ready, the line was put over the outrigger roller and with one man sailing the skiff, the other dipped the crabs feeding on the bait as the line was lifted to the surface by the roller. With motor boats replacing sail, a single man both runs the boat and dips the crabs. The present day dipnet is made of chicken wire which always remains open and will not foul on the crab's claws and legs when he is dropped into a barrel.

The crab pot is a box about 2 feet cube made entirely of chicken wire, divided into upper and lower halves with a bait compartment in the lower half. Crabs enter the pot through two funnel-shaped openings in the lower half and when they try to escape pass up through two more funnels into the upper half. The top may be opened for removing the catch. A line and buoy are attached to the pot. These are legal only in the Bay itself and the number one man may use is restricted. An open season for taking crabs is fixed in Maryland to protect brood crabs, but no such protection is given in Virginia. A small dredge called a scrape for taking crabs is used in Virginia and near Crisfield, Maryland.

Soft crabs, like cove oysters are caught one by one with a long handled dipnet, the bag of which is made of cotton netting for flexibility against the bottom. The crabber, standing in the bow of his boat, poles with the butt of the net handle and as he sees a crab, dips him up. Many are also caught in scrapes. If in a soft stage, the crab is put into a box of eel grass for shipment to market; if in peeler, shedder, or buster stages, the crabs are placed in separate containers, and transferred to floats to await shedding or sale. It is difficult to realize that about 3,000,000 pounds of soft crabs are annually caught and marketed by such methods. Until railroads were built down the Eastern Shore in the 1880's and ice became available, the only sale for soft crabs was in the locality where they were caught. Today "quick frozen" they may be had anywhere in the world.

Commercial fin fishing in the Chesapeake Bay has never attained either the size or the romantic nostalgia given the New England fisheries. In colonial days some small shipments of pickled sturgeon, caviar, pickled oysters and small quantities of salted fish were exported but the volume cannot be compared with the exports from Massachusetts. Before polution of the waters and the construction of power dams either killed the fish or cut off their spawning grounds, great runs of shad and herring entered the Bay each spring. Every river had local fame for the excellence of its fish, but the Potomac and the Susquehanna had some national celebrity. Huge catches of shad for food and herring for both food and fertilizer were made. A plantation which included a favorable shore for fishing was considered to have an asset of real importance, and some specialized gear was developed. Where a natural fishery existed haul seines, drift or set nets were used, with the catch pulled up onto the beach. Where such a shore was lacking, a battery, a large raft, was used to land the fish. The haul seine is a net from a couple of hundred to a couple of thousand feet long. It is set with one end on shore and the other carried by boat in a great circular sweep back to the starting point. The men then haul the net ashore with the fish caught in the bight. The haul seines were set from a galley, a large many oared flat bottomed boat with a large platform on the stern for the net. The gilling skiff was used with the set or drift nets, each fish being disentangled individually from the meshes. Set nets are attached to stakes driven into the bottom; drift nets, kept afloat by glass, cork, or wooden floats, are simply put into the water and allowed to drift with the tide with one end attached to the boat.

Today most of the food fish are caught in pound nets or weirs and the fish sold fresh. Weirs are a long, perhaps a mile or more, series of piles extending out from shore with a net strung between. This line, called a "leader," forces the fish to swim along it and at its end there is a pound, or trap, into which they swim. Once in, the fish cannot find its way out. At intervals the trap is emptied into a boat, and after being sorted the fish are iced and shipped to market. Weirs were first used by the Indians, and from them the settlers learned the art.

The only fishery in the Bay in which a large vessel enters is that for menhaden, a tiny sardine-like fish which feeds near the surface in huge schools. While of no direct value for humans, it provides an important oil, fertilizer, and proteins for animal food. Within the Bay the fishery is confined to Virginia waters, centering around Reedville. The fishery is said to have been started soon after the Civil War by one man who with a row boat and a small purse seine, caught fish which his wife tryed out in a kettle over an open fire. The oil was sold for industrial use and the residue, called meal, as fertilizer. In time the row boat became a pungy and the iron pot a small boiler. Today millions are invested in steel, diesel powered, especially designed vessels, and in large factories where only the smell of processing fish is wasted. Since the fish are to be found only in spring and summer, close inshore, and must be processed soon after they are caught, there is little chance of much romance here to compete with the whaling or Grand Banks fishing of New England. Only one phase of its work, one just discovered, has any public appeal: the chanties of the negro fishermen, which are as distinctive as any of the world's folk songs.

Oyster dredge fleet off Poplar Island, 1950. Photograph by H. Robins Hollyday.

Oyster dredgers at shucking house, Cambridge, Maryland, 1904. Photograph by Raymond Spears.

Bugeyes selling oysters in Baltimore, ca. 1890. Photograph owned by The United States National Museum.

Schooner *Kate McNamara* buying oysters, 1900. Photograph owned by John G. Earle.

Tonger selling oysters to a buy boat, 1915. Photograph by C. Lowndes Johnson.

Tonging fleet, 1950. Photograph by H. Robins Hollyday.

Tonger at work. Photograph by H. Robins
Hollyday.

Nippering oysters, Fishing Creek, Maryland,
1950. Photograph by M. V. Brewington.

Maryland Oyster Police schooner *Frolic.* Photograph by C. Lowndes Johnson.

Trot lining for hard crabs, Fishing Creek, Maryland, 1948. Tow-boat stern boat.

Box stern boat trot lining, Fishing Creek, Maryland, 1948.

Duck-tail stern Hooper's Island boat, Cambridge Creek, Maryland, 1950.

Crab shedding floats. Wenona, Maryland, 1935. Photograph by M. V. Brewington.

Indians fishing, crabbing, and oystering, 1585. Engraving from drawing by John White, published in Hariot: *Virginia*.

Shad galley laying out a net, Susquehanna River, Maryland, about 1902. Photograph owned by M. V. Brewington.

Shad nets and fishing batteries in Susequehanna River, Maryland, about 1890. A sloop, bushwack skiff, gilling skiff, and a pungy. Photograph owned by The United States National Museum.

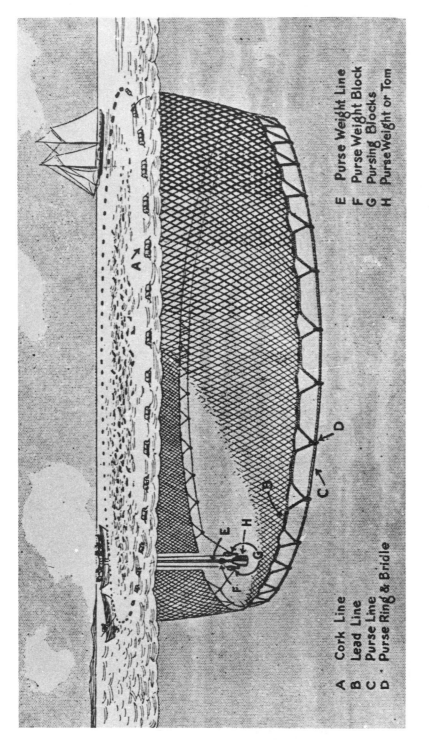

A   Cork Line
B   Lead Line
C   Purse Line
D   Purse Ring & Bridle

E   Purse Weight Line
F   Purse Weight Block
G   Pursing Blocks
H   Purse Weight or Tom

Diagram of a purse seine.   Photograph owned by The Mariners'
Museum.

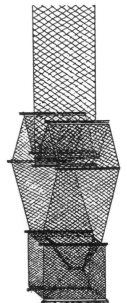

Diagram of a pound net.   From Graumont and Wenstrom: *Fisherman's
Knots and Nets.*

Caught swiping fish. Loon entangled in a pound net. Photograph by H. Robins Hollyday.

Eastern Shore caviar—herring roe being prepared for canning. Photograph by H. Robins Hollyday.

Menhaden steamer *William S. Brusstar*, of Reedville, Virginia, built at Baltimore, 1902. **Photo**-graph by Robert H. Burgess.

Pursing a seine.

Menhaden fishermen hauling a seine and shantying.

Chow for the fishermen. Photographs by William T. Radcliffe, 1948.

Haul seining for shad on Potomac River. Photograph from the U. S. Fish and Wildlife Service.

XI.

Pilots

OF COURSE there was no pilot to meet the Virginia colonists when they arrived off the Capes of Chesapeake. But from that day on there was always one man who knew the channels more thoroughly than his fellows. The first recorded pilot was John Clarke, who incidentally acted as pilot on the *Mayflower*, thirteen years after Jamestown was founded. In 1660 Bay pilotage was recognized by an act of the Virginia House of Burgesses which thereafter established the profession's qualifications, remuneration, and working conditions.

In addition to conning vessels the early Virginia pilots also had charge of buoying their part of the Bay and its tributaries, a job they continued long after the Federal government assumed such work. During the various wars which touched the Bay, the pilots usually suffered by at least capture and detention and frequently were forced to serve the enemy. Up to the outbreak of the Civil War the Virginia pilots were made official ship searchers for fugitive or stolen slaves. In 1852 the Maryland pilots formed an association for the protection of their livelihood against hostile legislation and ship owners. After the Civil War the Virginia pilots found carpet-baggers usurping their business and formed an association of their own. Except in an emergency the pilots of one State do not work in the waters of the other. When the Chesapeake and Delaware Canal was opened to deep-sea traffic in 1936, the Maryland pilots were given the task of conducting vessels into Baltimore and other Bay ports by this "backdoor."

By 1737 when its appearance was first recorded the Virginia pilot-boat had become a recognized and well-known type of watercraft out of which the famous Baltimore Clipper evolved. These boats, steadily growing in size but retaining the original model, were used exclusively until 1880 when the Maryland pilots built their first steamer, the *Pilot*. Now all the boats of both associations are mechanized to the point of complete air-conditioning in some instances. But whatever comforts the pilots can get they deserve for at best theirs is a hazardous profession on which rests the safety of the whole foreign trade of the Bay ports.

Four years after the first light house in North America, Boston Light, began operations in 1717, the Governor of Virginia urged the British Board of Trade to build one to mark the Bay entrance. The merchants of Maryland gladly joined but for political and economic reasons both at home and in Britain, the first Bay light, that on Cape Henry, was not opened until 1791, and then by the Federal government. Almost another century passed before the Bay was completely marked by lights and buoys.

Cape Charles Lightship. Photograph owned by The Peabody Museum.

Virginia pilot-boat *Mary* of Norfolk. Acquatint after Captain George R. Tobin, R.N., 1795. Owned by M. V. Brewington.

H.M.S. *Cleopatra* towing H.M.S. *Thetis* with the Virginia pilot-boat *Sally* of Norfolk in the foreground. Water color by Captain George R. Tobin, R.N., 1795 owned by The National Maritime Museum.

Bark *Winifred* of Richmond, Virginia, built by John Abrahams, Baltimore 1857, with Baltimore pilot-boat *Comet* off Cape Henry. Oil painting owned by The Merchants Club.

Maryland pilot-boat *Commerce* of Baltimore, about 1850. Water color owned by The Maryland Historical Society.

Virginia pilot-boat reefed. Water color, ca. 1800, owned by Harry Shaw Newman.

Maryland pilot-boat *Calvert*, built 1873, the last sailing pilot-boat out of Baltimore. Photograph owned by The Peale Museum.

Cape Henry Light, 1791, the first on Chesapeake
Bay. Photograph by Virginia State Chamber of
Commerce.

Typical screw-pile light, Windmill Point, Rappahannock River, Virginia.
Photograph by Robert H. Burgess.

XII.

Privateering, Piracy and War

PRIVATEERING is an old Chesapeake Bay custom that in some forms still continues when Virginians take oysters illegally in Maryland waters and Marylanders reciprocate by catching crabs in Virginia waters. It began in 1635 with William Claiborne granting to Phillip Taylor a letter of marque and reprisal against Lord Baltimore who had seized one of Claiborne's pinnaces trading without license in Maryland waters. From then through the Civil War it continued with legal sanction. Privateering reached its greatest activity during the War for Independence when Maryland commissioned over 248 and Virginia over 63; and during "Baltimore's Own War" in 1812 when over 12 Virginia and 126 Maryland vessels sailed with commissions or letters of marque. In both wars Bay vessels, usually clipper-type vessels of high speed and light armament, infested the British trade lanes taking a large but unknown number of prizes. Not all the private armed vessels managed to come home and many a crew found itself in British prisons. When the War of 1812 ended many of Baltimore's privateersmen transferred their operations and flags to the various South American countries then in revolt against Spain. Maryland with a governor of Unionist sympathies backed by plenty of troops sent out no privateers when the Confederacy authorized them, and Virginia had little chance to do so since the Union blockading squadrons easily closed the Bay. One privateer, the Baltimore pilot-boat *York,* did sail with a Virginia commission but seemingly accomplished little.

Just where privateering stopped and piracy began was difficult to decide even in the Seventeenth Century. Whatever the name the Chesapeake with its richly ladened shipping had more than its share. Pirates attempted to seize the Lord Proprietor and the Provincial magazine in 1681 but forewarned the raid was prevented by an especially strong guard thrown around the plantation. Based in North Carolina and Pennsylvania with the tacit consent of the governor of each, pirates intercepted shipping off the Capes and frequently within the Bay itself. Henry Every alias Bridgeman of the 46 gun ship *Fancy;* Captain Day of the brigantine *Josiah,* the well known Kidd, Captain Shelly of the ship *Nassau,* and Teach, the notorious Blackbeard, were all too close to the Capes for comfort and helped themselves to its shipping at will. But the Bay's own pirate was Roger Makeele. About 1685 he was making the Bay trade as dangerous as Blackbeard later made the deep-sea trade. Hiding in the low marshy islands that stretched south from his home on the Little Choptank, Makeele, his lieutenant aptly named Slaughter, and a gang of thirteen men and four women, watched for small craft in the Bay channels. These they took and carried into one of the islands, where they enjoyed themselves "drinking and feasting with Rumm or Brandy mutton Turkeys &C." Eventually the Governor of Virginia caught most of the gang and brought them to trial, but of Makeele no mention was made and it must be assumed he escaped the gallows. Piracy under the guise of Tory activity was rife during the War for Independence with raids on the Bayside homes of the well-to-do planters a frequent occurrence, Edward Lloyd's Wye among them. The last "bloody" pirate (the "oyster" variety still abounds) seems to have been a French schooner which in 1807 was captured by a group of volunteers from Baltimore.

Almost without exception every war in which England was involved had echoes within the Bay. In Britain's Civil War, Virginia at first loyal, allowed her Roundheads to migrate to Maryland where religious toleration offered sanctuary. Then when Parliament's commissioners took control of Virginia, she used these same Roundheads as a Fifth Column. The two forces, the Roundheads with naval reinforcement by a New England ship named the *Golden Lyon,* met on the banks of the Severn River and Baltimore's loyalists were defeated. During the second (1664) and third (1673) Anglo-Dutch Wars, Dutch squadrons raided the James River, capturing or destroying the tobacco fleets. Protection by the Royal Navy within the Bay and for ocean convoys was at once demanded by the tobacco merchants. In time and after much difficulty escort vessels were made available, and two or three times a year great fleets made up in the lower Bay and with one or more naval vessels sailed for home. For a century the system was continued upon each fresh outbreak of war. England's many wars with France down to 1763 always brought enemy privateers and sometimes men of war to the Capes. When the War for Independence began, Virginia's Royal Governor, Lord Dunmore, led a Tory fleet which seconded by Royal Naval vessels, cruised up and down the Bay, capturing vessels, looting and burning Bayside plantations. Each State organized a navy of its own, and although the bloodiest naval action of the war, the Battle of the Barges, took place in Tangier Sound, the State navies accomplished very little and usually were on the defensive. Howe's capture of the capital of the colonies, Philadelphia, in a campaign which foreshadowed the Japanese attack on Singapore began by way of the Chesapeake, entering the back door and avoiding the heavily fortified Delaware River. So complete was the British control of the Bay that Jefferson then governor of Virginia was unable to get advise boats across it with dispatches. Later the strategic position of the Bay was demonstrated by the engagement between the British and French fleets off the Capes in 1781 in which the British were forced to withdraw to New York enabling Washington to bottle up and take Cornwallis at Yorktown, a victory which virtually ended the War. Again in 1812 the Bay became almost a British lake with an entire army encamped on Tangier Island. In four months in 1813 they took 129 prizes within the Bay. Control of the sea and the Bay enabled them to lay seige to Norfolk, burn Washington, and the Library of Congress, loot many Bay towns and attempt to take Baltimore. Because Baltimore's privateers did British shipping so much damage and one commander, Thomas Boyle of the *Chasseur*, issued in London a derisive paper blockade of the British Isles, His Britannic Majesty's government and forces displayed a particular hatred towards the city. Their newspapers proclaimed that "the truculent inhabitants of Baltimore must be tamed with the weapons that shook the turrets of Copenhagen," and forewarned, Baltimore made preparations. On Sunday 11 September 1814, the signal station on Federal Hill sighted the British fleet: 4 ships of the line, 10 frigates, 5 bomb vessels, 1 rocket ship, plus tenders and transports. The alarm guns banged and the city's civilian soldiers left their church pews for battle posts. The Sunday before at their camp on Tangier Island, the British had been mustered for church before embarking. Joshua Thomas, the Methodist Parson of the Islands, knowing what was afoot had addressed them foretelling of their defeat. Now his prophecy was about to come true. Their army landed exactly where General Samuel Smith, Baltimore's commander, expected. The British general was killed almost at once by sharpshooters and his second made little progress against Smith's well conceived earthworks. Meanwhile the bomb vessels and the secret weapon, the rocket ship, moved in to knock to bits Fort McHenry, the principal harbor fort, with their 200 pound bomb shells and their devastating rockets. Once the fort was taken the city could be brought under the full fire of the fleet while the army attacked the rear. At 2 A. M. Tuesday the bombardment began, continuing until 6 A. M. Wednesday. That night on the deck of a cartel down harbor where he had gone to attempt the release of a prisoner of war stood Mr. Francis Scott Key. Throughout the night he heard the bombs burst over the fort, and as the rockets lighted the skies, he watched to see if the fort had lowered its flag in surrender. With dawn's first light he saw the flag still flying and knew the British were licked and in a mood of exalted patriotic fervor on the back of an old paper Key wrote a poem, *The Star Spangled Banner*. On 15 September the British army had been reembarked and their fleet was standing down the river: the turrets of Baltimore were unshaken and its inhabitants as truculent as ever—the only major city on the Atlantic Coast never held by a foreign enemy. For a few months the war dragged on but just as the Battle of Yorktown in the lower Bay had brought an end to the War for Independence, so the Battle of Baltimore in the upper Bay brought the end of the war for Free Trade and Sailor's Rights.

During the Civil War the Bay was constantly patrolled by Union vessels in an unsuccessful effort to prevent blockade running: a steady stream of sailing canoes sneaked out of the Eastern Shore rivers loaded with Southern sympathizers, quinine, and other drugs, landing anywhere in Virginia. Only one major naval action took place, but it changed the whole course of naval history, the engagement between the iron clads *Monitor* and *Virginia* (*Merrimac*).

But the longest war—it began in 1634 and still continues sporadically—has been that between Virginia and Maryland over the use of the Bay's waters. Generally this war has been one of words but at times every weapon from sword and match lock to automatic and plane have been used and the blood of both sides has darkened the waters. The first outbreak came when Baltimore seized one of Claiborne's vessels trading in Maryland without a license. Claiborne retaliated by dispatching his pinnace with a letter of marque. Baltimore's vessels caught her in Pocomoke Sound and took her. Then Baltimore sent an amphibious expedition against Claiborne's posts on Kent and Palmer Islands and captured both. Claiborne bided his time for several years and regained his posts but in a word battle eventually lost them, forever. Next came attempts by Virginia to force vessels loading in the Potomac River which to its South bank is owned by Maryland, to enter and clear in Virginia custom houses, and later Virginia attempted to lay a tax on Maryland vessels passing through the Capes. Rather than start another quarrel, Maryland by treaty allowed Virginians the use of the fisheries in the Potomac and Virginia gave up all pretenses of taxing Maryland vessels, a right which the Federal Constitution would have denied her anyway. Both states have prohibited the citizens of the other from oystering and crabbing in its waters, except the Potomac. In the 1880's when oystering was highly profitable and the oyster fleets were in the hands of a lawless group, a fleet of Maryland vessels invaded the Rappahannock River, threatening to burn the country-side if the inhabitants interferred with dredging. When the news reached Richmond the governor called out an infantry company and one of artillery and embarked them on two steamers at Norfolk. By a ruse the steamers got above the oystermen dredging in the river and with guns blazing started an attack. His Excellency captured all except one schooner. In the mêlée she started down the Bay with all sail set before a spanking breeze. The governor's steamer followed in chase. For forty miles sail outran steam; then the wind failed and the governor made his prize. But what prizes: all the vessels were Virginia owned; the Maryland fleet had departed up the Bay the night before. Similar episodes have occurred several times in each State and as recently as the late 1940's a Virginia aerial patrolman killed a Maryland crabber who it was alleged was working in Virginia waters. A Virginia jury is said to have acquitted the patrolman and a Maryland jury to have indicted him for murder. Probably the war will continue as long as an oyster or crab is left in the Bay and the other side of the boundary looks greener.

Ship *Sphinx* of Baltimore and other American vessels aiding a British East Indiaman beat off a French frigate, 1800. Water color by Captain Louis Brantz of the *Sphinx*, owned by The Peabody Museum, Salem.

Privateer schooner *Dolphin* of Baltimore in action with British ship *Hebe* and a brig, 1813. Colored lithograph from Cogeshall: *History of the American Privateers.*

The famous Baltimore clipper brig *Chasseur* in action with H.M. schooner *St. Lawrence*, 1815. Colored lithograph from Cogeshall: *History of the American Privateers.*

Letter of marque schooner *Catch Me Who Can* of Dorchester County, Maryland, escaping from a British armed brig, 1815. Acquatint by W. J. Huggins, owned by The National Maritime Museum.

Baltimore clipper privateer schooner. Oil painting by Burton, 1815, owned by The National Maritime Museum.

Privateer *Surprize* of Baltimore, capturing the British ship *Star*, 1815. Water color owned by The Peabody Museum, Salem.

Confederate privateer *York,* late a Baltimore pilot-boat. Water colored drawing by John Wilcox owned by The Maryland Historical Society.

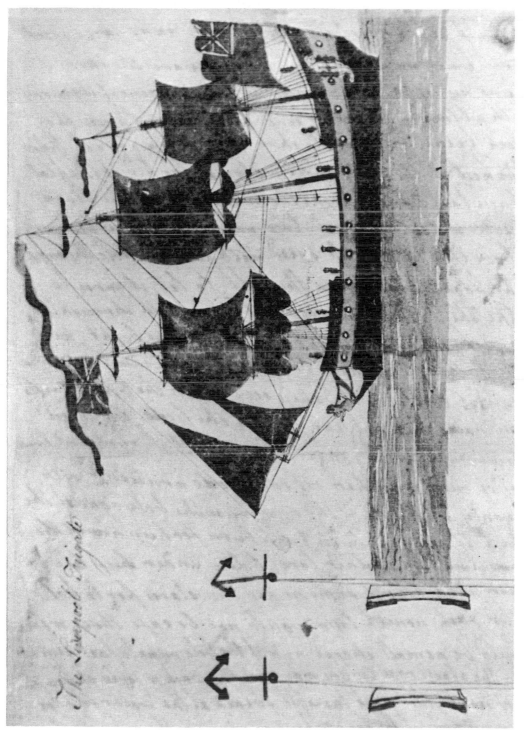

Riley's plan to burn British men of war attacking Annapolis by pulling small boats full of burning wood and tar against the ships' sides. Ink drawing by Jeremiah Riley, owned by The Hall of Records.

Captain William Stone of Maryland with his command, the Continental sloop *Hornet*, in the background. Oil painting by Charles Willson Peale. Photograph from Office of Naval Records and History.

The Continental sloop *Hornet*, 1776, a detail from the Stone portrait.

Before we had a navy, foreign ships used the Chesapeake as a handy rendezvous. Here three British men of war are anchored in Lynnhaven Roads. Water color by Captain George R. Tobin, R.N., 1795, owned by The National Maritime Museum.

The action between Baltimore's own frigate the U.S.S. *Constellation* and the French frigate *L'Insurgent*, 1799. Engraving by Edward Savage. Photograph from Office of Naval Records and History.

The burning of Havre de Grace by the British Navy in the War of 1812. Colored engraving owned by The Maryland Historical Society.

British rocket ship of the type which attacked Fort McHenry. Colored etching, dated 1814, in The National Maritime Museum.

The Bombardment of Fort McHenry, 13 Sept. 1814. The house left foreground and vessel in frame are at Salenave's shipyard. Colored engraving by J. Bower, owned by The Peale Museum.

The U.S.S. *Cumberland* being sunk by the C.S.S. *Virginia (Merrimac.)* Colored lithograph, owned by The United States Navy Dept.

THANK YOU FOR YOUR ORDER   MR KEN S DORR

ORDER NO.

1982280101

BACK ORDER	CANCEL	LOCATION	PICKED	ITEM	ITEM NO.
1		B0735		WHALE SHIPS AND WHALING	029510
2		B17A5		CHESAPEAKE BAY	094371
3					
4					
5					
6					
7					
8					
9					
10					
11					
12					
13					
14					
15					
16					
17					
18					

7 SEP 12 1974

FROM: PUBLISHERS CENTRAL BUREAU   34 ENGELHARD AVENUE   AVENEL N. J. 07001

The engagement between the *Merrimac* and *Monitor*. Lithograph after Charles Worret, an eye witness, owned by The Mariners' Museum.

Blackbeard the Pirate. Engraving by B. Cole in The Mariners' Museum.

XIII.

The Bay's Maritime Museums

SINCE only in very recent years has the Chesapeake region become conscious of its maritime history, it is not generally recognized that few areas of comparable size have done quite so much toward the preservation of nautical art and antiquities. There are five museums with extensive marine exhibits on permanent display and others which periodically pay considerable attention to the field.

The most venerable is The United States National Museum in Washington with a large collection illustrating the history of watercraft of all types with special attention given to American developments. Among its holdings are a group of builders' half-models and rigged models of both small and large vessels built around the Bay. Many of these were gathered by the United States Fish Commission and because of their age, provenance, and generally excellent condition are of great historical importance. The Museum also has a number of pieces of Bay carved work, a large collection of photographs of vessels and work scenes, and the plans of many Bay-built vessels are included with those drawn by The Historic American Merchant Marine Survey.

In Washington also is The Naval Historical Foundation's Truxtun-Decatur Museum, the youngest of the region's maritime collections. Housed in beautifully designed rooms in an outbuilding on the property which Commodore Stephen Decatur, Jr., acquired with his War of 1812 prize money, the Museum changes its entire exhibits several times each year. Among its holdings is the Eberstadt Print Collection, one of the most important in both quantity and quality in the world.

Almost exclusively naval is The Museum of The United States Naval Academy at Annapolis. Here is to be found the great Rogers Collection of ship models which contains many of the finest existing admiralty models; the Robinson Collection of Naval Prints; and a vast assemblage of relics and memorabilia of the naval service from its beginnings to the present.

At The Maryland Historical Society in Baltimore is to be found displayed a small group of paintings, builder's and rigged models, and objects relating particularly to Maryland's part in Chesapeake Bay history. Due to lack of space the greater part of the holdings are not on exhibit, but in the near future an especially designed building will be constructed to house the maritime collection. The Society's library holds an extensive collection of manuscript materials concerned with the shipping and maritime trades, logs and account books, and a large print collection.

While The Peale Museum in Baltimore has no permanent marine exhibition, it has a fine collection of Chesapeake Bay paintings, models and objects and an unrivaled collection of Baltimore prints and photographs.

Largest of all and one of the world's great maritime museums is The Mariners' Museum at Newport News, Virginia. In its tremendous collections is a very large group of Chesapeake Bay materials of all types. A few words cannot even outline the scope of its library or its holdings of pictorial materials, models, and objects on every phase of maritime activity.

Sign of Tarbell's Tavern in Norfolk, Virginia. Owned by The Mariners' Museum.

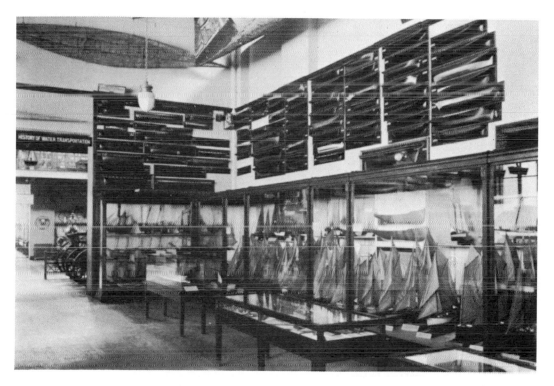

The United States National Museum, Watercraft Collection. Photograph from The Museum.

A portion of the Truxtun-Decatur Museum. Photograph from The Museum.

The United States Naval Academy, part of main exhibition room. Official United States Navy photograph.

One of the marine collection rooms, The Maryland Historical Society. Photograph from The Society.

The entrance gallery of The Mariners' Museum. Photograph from The Museum.

Portion of a special Chesapeake Bay Exhibit at The Mariners' Museum.
Photograph from the Museum.

XIV.

Sport

FROM the Mid-Seventeenth Century Lord Baltimore had a series
of what were sometimes referred to as yachts. Commanded
by the Admiral of Maryland, one vessel was ship rigged and named
for His Lordship, *Baltimore*. Another, rig unknown, was named the
Loyal Charles. They may have carried the Governor about the Bay
from time to time on pleasure junkets, but actually they were more
coast guards since they were frequently ordered to cruise from the
Potomac to the Head of the Bay ". . . for the security of his Lops
Province from . . . Robbers, Pyrates, Spies, or others." Real pleasure
boating, though, had appeared by 1689 when Major Robert Sewall
had the ketch *Susanna* in commission. Since then the Bay has been
steadily used by yachtsmen, and every great plantation owner and
many officials of both provinces had pleasure craft. Robert Carter of
Nomini, for instance, owned the schooner *Harriet;* Edward Lloyd had
a magnificent schooner; Lord Dunmore, Governor of Virginia, cruised
on the *Lady Gower;* even George Washington, poor sailor though he
was, owned at least two sailing vessels. Barges rowed by slaves with
stern-sheet canopies for the ladies and gentlemen were commonplace
for journeys to church or to visit friends. Organized regattas were
being held by 1760. A century later the racing of work boats, particularly canoes and skiffs, was widespread and has continued down to the
present. The Bay's first yacht club (the word being used to mean a
group or club of persons who joined to build or own a pleasure boat)
seems to have come into existence in 1852. The Bay's first club of
yachtsmen in the present sense of the word was organized in 1885,
on board the yacht *Gaetina*, The Chesapeake Bay Yacht Club of Easton,
Maryland. It flourished and still does.

Even before Izaak Walton began his angling expeditions in the
English streams, Virginia had his forerunner, the Reverend Mr. Alexander Whitaker who was busy working over the Virginia waters, both
catching and writing about the "daintie fish" that he could not ". . .

give proper names to . . . I have caught with mine angle, Pike, Carps, Eele, Perches of sixe severall kindes . . ." Doubtless before Mr. Whitaker and certainly since him, pleasure fishing has been one of the Bay's leading attractions. Just about 1800 one party was described:

> "Last Saturday returned from the Capes of Chesapeake [to Easton] the schooner Dolphin, Capt. Ewing, on board of which went a number of Gentlemen on a party of pleasure, who having a seine and a variety of fishing tackle was abundantly supplied with fish such as Skate, Flounder, Fluke, Trout, Perch, Mullet, Drum, Sheepshead, Mackeral, Hogfish, Dogfish, Crabs, Oysters, Cockles, Doublehead pike etc., etc. . . . and to crown their felicity, they found no vessel in the bay able to sail with them."

So great has been the appeal of rod and reel that it has become a big business. In 1936 an annual contest was organized, the Chesapeake Bay Fishing Fair, which also serves as an association of sportsmen and guides for the protection and improvement of the sport. The first contest drew 35 boats and about 160 anglers; fourteen years later 1900 anglers registered and about 12,000 persons came to see the fun.

Fishing is certainly the leading sport around the Bay, but close to it is ducking. Captain John Smith was the first writer to comment upon it. "In Winter there are great plentie of Swans, Cranes, Herons, Geese, Brants, Ducks, Wigeon . . . Of all these sorts great abundance, and some other strange kinds, to us unknown . . ." Lord Baltimore's colonists were told to carry with them "Fowling-pieces . . . Powder and Shott and Flint Stones . . ." But in those days while the early settlers may have taken much pleasure in ducking, it was primarily a means of getting food and not a very difficult means when flocks seven miles long were seen over the Bay, and John Smith killed 148 in three shots. Not until quick and easy transportation was available did ducking become a sport with hunters coming from the Eastern cities and in no time a business of providing guides, decoys, dogs, and other equipment developed. Market hunting with its terrible slaughter of water fowl came too and the supposedly inexhaustible flocks began to diminish noticeably. Legislation to give the game some protection then became necessary: open seasons were started, the fire arms used by the market hunters were restricted, bag limits were imposed, and certain methods of hunting were prohibited. As the huge flocks began to decrease and the birds became more wary some method of bringing the game closer to the hunter's gun became necessary and the old Indian trick of using decoys was reborn. It is recorded in 1814 that hunters were using "... wooden figures, cut and painted so as to represent ducks ..." Eventually a hunter required as many as 500 decoys, and from that need grew the decoy making business. At one time there were fourteen professionals at Havre de Grace. A few are still working by hand methods, meticulously painting the wooden birds with a precision that fools not only the ducks but also many an ornithologist. Dogs, too, are needed and Bay ducking gave the world one of the greatest of all breeds, happily named for the area, the Chesapeake Retriever. No dog has greater intelligence, none greater natural aptitude, and none greater enjoyment of its work. It can be definitely established that the breed originated from a pair of Newfoundlands which were saved from a wreck and brought to Maryland in 1807. These were bred to water spaniels and from these litters, one of which was born on the Western and one on the Eastern Shore, came the Chesapeake.

Pleasure Boats.

The subscriber presents his compliments to his customers and the public for the liberal encouragement received last year, and informs them that he means to continue to furnish **PLEASURE BOATS** of the first quality for boarding vessels, or for excursions of pleasure any where this side of Annapolis on the shortest notice. He will also, within the above-mentioned limits, go up and across the bay; and in conclusion will go to the Fish House, Fort, Lazaretto, or capt. Melvin's—Apply to near Capt. Case's wharf, No. 1, the corner of Philpot and Thames sts Fell's Point, to

ap 22 ws   JILES WILLIAMS.

Baltimore's first ad for pleasure craft, 1824. From the *Baltimore American*.

Cambridge Yacht Club Annual Regatta. Photograph by H. Robins Hollyday.

Power boat races, Miles River Yacht Club, St. Michaels, Maryland. Photograph by H. Robins Hollyday.

Free for all sailing race: skiffs, stars, canoes, a large schooner yacht. Photograph by H. Robins Hollyday.

"Standing start" of a work canoe race, St. Michaels, Maryland, about 1895. Photograph owned by John G. Earle.

Log canoe racing off St. Michaels, Maryland, 1930. Photograph by H. Robins Hollyday.

Ducking from a sink-box, Wye River, Maryland. Photograph by C. Lowndes Johnson.

Sink-box gunner. Photograph by C. Lowndes Johnson.

Guns of the market duck hunter. Top: punt gun with ram rod and worm for withdrawing loads in the barrel; normal 12-gauge gun; a second punt gun. Bottom L. to R.: four barrel battery gun; two 4-gauge guns. Photograph from The United States Wild Life Service.

Chesapeake Bay dog *Champion Barrum*. Oil painting by J. M. Tracy (1843-1893), courtesy, E. J. Rousuck.

Soft crabbing, fun and profit for man and beast. Photograph by M. V. Brewington.

Rail bird shooting on the Patuxent River. Photographs by Frank A. Moorshead, Jr.

Canoe sails shifted to ice boats in the old days at St. Michaels. Photograph by
Thomas Sewall, ca. 1900.

One of the first motor boats on Miles River—the oars on the canopy were often needed
to get home. Photographs by Thomas Sewall.

The Floating Theater. Photograph by A. C. Brown, 1938.

Rehearsal. Photograph by Tom Firth

Index

Format and jacket designed by G. William Kirschenhofer, lithography by Universal Lithographers, Inc., composition by Modern Linotypers, Inc. and Baltimore Type & Composition Corp., binding by Moore & Co., Inc., all of Baltimore, Md. Lithographed on 70 lb. Silkote, manufactured by S. D. Warren Company.